CHARACTER
out of
Chaos

CHARACTER
out of
Chaos

DARING *to be a* DANIEL
in TODAY'S WORLD

DAVID O. DYKES

Kregel
Publications

Character out of Chaos: Daring to be a Daniel in Today's World

© 2004 by David O. Dykes

Published by Kregel Publications, a division of Kregel, Inc., P.O. Box 2607, Grand Rapids, MI 49501.

Unless otherwise indicated, Scripture quotations are from the *Holy Bible, New International Version*®. NIV®. © 1973, 1978, 1984 by International Bible Society. Used by permission of Zondervan Publishing House. All rights reserved.

Scripture quotations marked NASB are from the *New American Standard Bible.* © 1960, 1962, 1963, 1968, 1971, 1972, 1973, 1975, 1977, 1994, the Lockman Foundation.

Scripture quotations marked THE MESSAGE are from *The Message.* © by Eugene Peterson, 1993, 1994, 1995. Used by permission of NavPress Publishing Group.

Scripture quotations marked NKJV are from the *New King James Version.* © 1979, 1980, 1982, Thomas Nelson, Inc., Publishers.

Scripture quotations marked KJV are from the Authorized King James Version.

Produced with the assistance of Fluency Organization, Inc.

Cover design: John M. Lucas

Library of Congress Cataloging-in-Publication Data
Dykes, David O.
    Character out of chaos: daring to be a Daniel in today's world / by David O. Dykes
        p.   cm.
Includes bibliographical references.
    1. Bible. O.T. Daniel—Criticism, interpretation, etc. 2. Daniel (Biblical figure) I. Title.
BS1555.52.D95 2004
224'.506—dc22   2004019312

ISBN 0-8254-2493-3

Printed in the United States of America

04 05 06 07 08 / 5 4 3 2 1

To
J. R. ("Coach") and Joanie Chafin.
I don't love you just as in-laws;
I love you as if you were my own mom and dad!

Contents

Introduction

The most significant crisis we face in our nation and families today is not economic or political—it is a crisis of character. The unsettling reality is that over the past forty years, we have seen the continual decline of moral and spiritual values in America gain momentum. In fact, if the historians who observe America repeating the social and moral trends of England almost one hundred years after the fact are right, we may be well on our way to becoming another great nation with more tourists than worshipers in its cathedrals and church buildings.

Until a tragic September day in 2001, America assumed that as the strongest nation on earth, other nations respected and admired us. Suddenly we learned that millions of people hate America. Many of us are still asking, "Why do these people hate us?" The answer is shocking but not so surprising. America has become the world's chief exporter of immorality, mainly through the media.

A nation that established principled government and freedom now leads the world in divorce, violence, and abortion on demand. Several years ago, I heard Billy Graham say, "If God does not judge America for her sins, He will owe an apology to Sodom and Gomorrah!" What happened to cause this moral decay? At the grassroots level, we have compromised our corporate commitment to character.

Although many people have turned to the Old Testament book of Daniel as a cornerstone in biblical prophecy, few have explored this book for what it teaches us about the importance of character and the powerful effect that an uncompromised life has on society. Coupled with his role as an extraordinary prophet, Daniel was foremost an ordinary person like us who faced challenges very similar to those we experience today.

Daniel grew up in a God-fearing culture. However, as a young man he was forced overnight into a godless society to live among the pagan Babylonians. Suffering from cultural whiplash, Daniel struggled with major uncertainties, religious persecution, fear, war, and rampant immorality.

His personal story mirrors many Christians' own experience. Today is a different world than yesterday, both morally and spiritually. Forty years ago, the "Leave It to Beaver" family was typical (except for the pearls Mrs. Cleaver wore while cleaning her house!). Mom and Dad were in their first marriage, and every evening they sat down for dinner with their two boys. In contrast, the typical twenty-first-century family doesn't look to the Cleavers, the Waltons, or the Ingalls for inspiration. Instead, it reveres and even closely resembles the free-spirited morality of the Osbourne family.

The movers and shakers in Daniel's new liberal culture assaulted his personal purity and relentlessly tempted him to compromise. Likewise, today's politicians, media moguls, sports figures, and other influential forces are feverishly working to spin morality and downplay its value. However, the problem isn't limited to Washington or Hollywood; the problem is within the human heart of every one of us. The crisis involves the foundation of everything we do—our character.

For all the similarities to our world today, Daniel's life stands out in dramatic contrast to mainstream culture. Through Daniel's stalwart faith, God transformed the chaos amid Daniel's immoral and crazed culture into opportunities to build his character and act on principle. We need God to help us perform under pressure and articulate our ethics in such a way that we inspire and influence others around us. At the same time, we need to see how prayer plays a significant role in buttressing our character and convictions when we are tempted.

Most importantly, we must remember that Daniel's story is a realistic one. He paid a price for daring to live without compromise, and so will we. Principled living often leads to high profile persecution. Daniel's prophecies remind us that the price never comes down for that kind of commitment. In fact, chaos will only increase as we approach the end times.

Those who dare to be a Daniel in today's world realize what's at stake and rest their hope in Christ's ultimate victory. America needs an army of daring Daniels today—men and women who recognize that the test of our character most often comes at a time we can least afford to fail.

Chapter One

Character in Crisis

But Daniel resolved not to defile himself with the royal food and wine, and he asked the chief official for permission not to defile himself this way. Now God had caused the official to show favor and sympathy to Daniel, but the official told Daniel, "I am afraid of my lord the king, who has assigned your food and drink. Why should he see you looking worse than the other young men your age? The king would then have my head because of you." Daniel then said to the guard whom the chief official had appointed over Daniel, Hananiah, Mishael and Azariah, "Please test your servants for ten days: Give us nothing but vegetables to eat and water to drink. Then compare our appearance with that of the young men who eat the royal food, and treat your servants in accordance with what you see." So he agreed to this and tested them for ten days. At the end of the ten days they looked healthier and better nourished than any of the young men who ate the royal food.

—Daniel 1:8–15

Daniel in a den of lions is one of the most popular Bible stories ever told. However, there never would have been a story about

Daniel in the *lion's den* (or any other equally well-known story about Daniel) without there having been the story of Daniel in the *dining room* when he was a teenager. Read Daniel 1:1–18, where the story begins with Daniel's deportation to Babylon. "In the third year of the reign of Jehoiakim king of Judah, Nebuchadnezzar king of Babylon came to Jerusalem and besieged it" (Dan. 1:1). That's how man would report it. But this is what God said was happening:

> And the Lord delivered Jehoiakim king of Judah into his hand, along with some of the articles from the temple of God. These he carried off to the temple of his God in Babylonia and put in the treasure house of his God. Then the king ordered Ashpenaz, chief of his court officials, to bring in some of the Israelites from the royal family and the nobility—young men without any physical defect, handsome, showing aptitude for every kind of learning, well informed, quick to understand, and qualified to serve in the king's palace. He was to teach them the language and literature of the Babylonians. (Dan. 1:2–4)

The "young men" in this passage were young teenagers, most of them twelve to fifteen years old. They were good-looking, smart guys—high on their ACT scores and upper profilers on the SAT. They were perfect specimens for the king's experiment. In other words, he wanted to immerse these Hebrew boys in a very different culture and see what happened.

Verse 5 informs us, "The king assigned them a daily amount of food and wine from the king's table." Not bad! The Babylonians offered to these teenagers the same food that the king ate and the same wine that he drank. However, these delicacies soon became delicate issues for Daniel.

They were to be trained for three years, and after that they were to enter the king's service. Among these were some from Judah: Daniel, Hananiah, Mishael, and Azariah. The chief official gave them new names: to Daniel, the name Belteshazzar; to Hananiah, Shadrach; to Mishael, Meshach; and to Azariah, Abednego. But Daniel resolved not to defile himself with the royal food and wine, and he asked the chief official for permission not to defile himself this way. Now God had caused the official to show favor and sympathy to Daniel, but the official told Daniel, "I am afraid of my lord the king, who has assigned your food and drink. Why should he see you looking worse than the other young men your age? The king would then have my head because of you." Daniel then said to the guard whom the chief official had appointed over Daniel, Hananiah, Mishael, and Azariah, "Please test your servants for ten days: Give us nothing but vegetables to eat. . . ." (Dan. 1:5–12)

The King James Version describes Daniel's request as "pulse." The word in Hebrew is *zeroim,* which means "food that comes from seeds," and it includes fruit, vegetables, and grain products. Realizing that such was not the usual fare of teenagers, especially those with the royal court chefs at their disposal, Daniel threw in a disclaimer regarding his request: "Compare our appearance with that of the young men who eat the royal food, and treat your servants in accordance with what you see" (Dan. 1:13).

So he [the official] agreed to this and tested them for ten days. At the end of the ten days they looked healthier and better nourished than any of the young men who ate the royal food. So the guard took away their choice food and the wine that they were to drink and gave them vegetables instead. To these four young men [teenagers] God gave knowledge and understanding of all

> kinds of literature and learning. And Daniel could understand
> visions and dreams of all kinds. . . . And Daniel remained there
> [in the palace] until the first year of King Cyrus [i.e., seventy
> years and four kings later]. (Dan. 1:14–17, 21)

After ten days, the physical elements of Daniel's diet caused the
boys to appear healthier and better nourished than the rest of the
king's academy. However, Daniel's food scruples were not the only
challenge he would face.

CHANGE IS DIFFICULT

Imagine Daniel's situation. He grew up a good Jewish boy in
Jerusalem. He studied faithfully the Scriptures of his forefathers,
went to the temple, and prayed to the God of Israel. Suddenly, a
foreign enemy conquered his nation. The Babylonians plucked
the teenage Daniel from his home and put him in a foreign envi-
ronment with a different language, people, and food. The
Babylonians announced to this naive boy, "You've got to become
a new person—starting today."

That's tough. Imagine what it's like to be exported suddenly to
a new culture where everyone is speaking another language. Some
of us might actually know what that is like. We know what it's like
to be transferred to a new position at work—even within the same
company—where we're two steps behind every deadline and
feeling clueless at team meetings. Some people know what it's like
to try to make a new life in a new town, where even a necessary
trip to an unfamiliar grocery store seems a challenge. As students,
we might have experienced the fear of transferring to a new school
where we didn't know anyone. Unfortunately, too many people
know about going to sleep in one world and waking up in the
next. It might be a world in which a meeting with the boss begins,

"I'm sorry to tell you this, but we're going to have to let you go." Or it might be a strange place where an otherwise typical dinner and a movie date with a mate ends with the announcement, "I just don't feel like I love you anymore."

YOUR GREATEST TRIAL

The greatest trial in life is to trust God in the midst of pain and difficulty. Daniel hadn't planned for this change—but he had a plan for dealing with it. Even as a young boy, Daniel relied on God's principles for living. No matter how his new culture tried to change him on the outside, Daniel's inner predisposition would remain unaltered. It was the one possession he took with him to this new world.

Now the question is, "Can we trust God when our world falls apart?" We might feel as though our world is falling apart because of the death of a loved one. Or maybe someone just received a doctor's report concerning cancer. Some of us have financial or family problems. Still others might have to make a tremendous decision but have no clue as to the answer.

It's easy to trust God when things are going great, when we can pay all of our bills, when our health is great, and when everybody loves us and we love those around us. But when the bottom falls out of our world, all of our plans for happiness seem to crumble with it. That's when the trial comes. That's when we feel like asking, "Does anybody really know what's going on? Who's got the plan around here?" Will we still trust God then? Daniel did, and we can too.

Although Daniel was in a completely different culture and a challenging new land, God was behind the scenes orchestrating it all. In fact, we can jump ahead to Daniel 2:28 to find the theme of the entire book: "There is a God in heaven who reveals mysteries." In other words, *God is in heaven, and He is in control.*

Your Greatest Temptation

The greatest temptation in life is to compromise our beliefs and convictions to be like everyone else. I call this cultural brainwashing. When we are at our most vulnerable point, when we don't have a sound plan for making it through life, the world has a ready-made plan waiting. The world's plan is a time-tested tradition, and we can count on its powerful vortex sucking us under—unless we resist.

What happened to the teenaged Daniel twenty-six hundred years ago is happening today to every child, teenager, college student, and adult who lives in the current godless culture. It pervades the music to which we listen, the television programs and movies we watch, and the magazines we read. This culture is trying to immerse us, brainwash us, and make us just like everybody else.

King Nebuchadnezzar was pretty shrewd. He knew that if he could change the minds and hearts of young people, he would have their allegiance forever. The values we hold and the decisions we make as teenagers often determine the rest of our lives. It's kind of scary when we consider the battles that teens already face with raging hormones inside their changing bodies. The decisions that teens make now have the potential to determine the rest of their lives—for better or worse. However, teenagers aren't the only ones to face this battle. Our culture considers everyone "up for grabs" when it comes to the battle for hearts and minds. The choice is ours. Here's what the Bible says about the world:

> Don't love the world's way, because love of the world squeezes out love for the Father. Practically everything that goes on in the world, wanting your own way, wanting everything for yourself, wanting to appear important, has nothing to do with the

Father. The world with all of its wanting, wanting, wanting is on the way out, but whoever does what God wants is set for eternity. (1 John 2:15–17 *The Message*)

Note that Daniel and the other three Hebrew boys weren't tortured to change. In fact, just the opposite occurred. Nebuchadnezzar used pampering, not persecution. He offered them extravagant food, seducing and enticing them to overindulge. That's still the world's most successful tactic. It doesn't try to make us be "real bad"; it tries to entice and overindulge us to the point that we don't have time for God anymore. The world wants to make us so busy doing all of the things that make up our "life" that we don't have time to get on our knees and pray. The world wants to keep us busy so we will have other things to do than care for ourselves spiritually. If the world does not persecute us outright, it seduces us. It entices us with all of the best that it has to offer.

Daniel had to make a firm choice to keep from compromising his spiritual convictions and becoming like everybody else in his culture. He met with three challenging crises and had to sift his responses through three important questions—the same three questions that we must answer today.

Authority Crisis: What Is Truth?

Daniel had to decide whether to believe God or the Babylonian culture. "What is truth?" Philosophers have struggled with this question for centuries. We initially face the question growing up at home as children and teenagers. Our parents try to tell us in one way or another, "This is right, and this is wrong. This is truth, and this is error." Those who grow up with any sort of religious training learn even more examples of truth and error, right and wrong. However, as a child grows out from under the direct influence of a parent, pastor, or religion, the once black-and-white issues start to shift into shades of gray. Music, friends, movies, and television introduce a new set of values—and these influences grow stronger as a teen becomes an adult. The world begins to say, "Hey, your beliefs aren't necessarily true. Why do you accept it just because your parents told you? Why do you accept it just because religion told you? Come on. Is it really truth?"

In America today, we have embraced moral relativism. The cultural attitude is that there's no such thing as *absolute* truth. I've heard that statement many times, and it causes me to wonder whether the person is *absolutely* certain there is no absolute truth. If someone is "absolutely" certain, the argument against absolute truth self-destructs.

People look at Christian beliefs and say, "That's *your* truth; that's not *my* truth." For example, because I believe the Bible, and because I'm not ashamed to stand up and say the Bible says that homosexual behavior is wrong, the culture calls me intolerant. Because I am willing to stand up and say the Bible teaches that abortion is murder, the culture brands me as an intolerant bigot, and such intolerant attitudes don't fit into the American culture. Because I claim the Bible says that there's only one way to heaven and that is Jesus Christ, our culture labels me as an intolerant bigot.

The only unforgivable sin in America today is intolerance; everything else is permissible. However, those who promote the anti-Bible, anti-family agenda are intolerant of those who affirm God's Word. Those who label others intolerant are often guilty of intolerance themselves. It's so warped that it's almost laughable!

However, the Bible clearly teaches that *there is absolute truth.* Some things are right for everyone at all times, and some things are wrong for everyone at all times. We must decide individually, "Am I going to believe the Word of God as my authority for living, or am I going to accept what my culture tells me?" Daniel faced this same first question. However, he also faced another question.

Identity Crisis: Who Am I?

Daniel's Hebrew name means literally "God is judge." The Hebrew names of Daniel's three companions—Hananiah, Mishael, Azariah—also described the God of Israel. However, once they moved to the Babylonian culture, they received substitute names that related to the pagan gods of Babylon. Daniel became Belteshazzar, which meant "servant of Baal," their lead pagan deity. However, we'll soon note that Daniel continued to be addressed as Daniel—even by the king himself.

In the same way, those who are willing to call themselves Christians in private must be willing to do so publicly as well. We must decide individually, "Am I willing to be called a Christian in our culture?" I believe a trend that started in the eighties will gain momentum in the twenty-first century. In our American culture, the label "born-again Christian" is going to take on an even more negative connotation. The identity "born-again Christian" will send a chill up our culture's spine. The culture will follow through on such confessions with labels of its own such as "right-wing conspiracy," "intolerance," and "bigotry."

This is not to say that cultural American Christians are not socially acceptable on many levels. Indeed they are. Yet, a biblical Christian and one who simply adopts a Christian label are vastly different. In fact, many people in our world today often identify America as a "Christian culture." However, those who refuse to cloak their convictions for the sake of social acceptability find themselves on the outskirts of popular opinion. Are we willing to identify ourselves as Christians?

Daniel faced a third and final question—a moral one. We must decide to dare to be like Daniel before we encounter an authority, identity, or moral crisis. We will succeed in a crisis only when we plan our response ahead of time.

Moral Crisis: How Will I Live?

King Nebuchadnezzar said to these Hebrew teenagers, "Young men, I will make you into good Babylonians. I'm going to be your new authority. Forget God; forget the Bible." That was their authority crisis. Next, he said, "I'm going to give you new names. Your name is not Daniel anymore; you will now represent the gods that I want you to represent." There was the identity crisis. Finally, King Nebuchadnezzar said, "Daniel, you have to eat my food; you have to drink my wine. After all, I'm your boss." That was Daniel's moral crisis.

"If only my moral crisis were so easy!" one might say. "Eating and drinking? What's the big deal?" In Daniel's day, food laws were no minor issue. According to the Old Testament, Jews could eat only food that was kosher. Daniel could not eat certain meats such as pork, camel, or beef that someone had sacrificed to idols. To Daniel, eating and drinking the king's food represented a rejection of God's commands. To obey the king, he would have to compromise his convictions. Minor compromises lead to major collapses.

In 1999, scientists studied a particular giant redwood tree that had been standing strong in the California forest for more than four hundred years. It had survived storms, lightning, earthquakes, and forest fires. However, without warning, this huge tree crashed to the floor of the forest. What happened to cause its demise? When scientists cut into the tree, they found thousands of tiny beetles had slowly eaten away at the heart of the tree.

In the scope of the whole Christian life, I'll agree eating and drinking is relatively insignificant. However, if we consistently make the wrong choices about the little things, we might experience a spiritual collapse from the inside. How often we try to trivialize an infraction, saying in effect, "It's no big deal." Just as Daniel's dilemma seemed to be "just food," we attempt to minimize a number of vices. For example, our culture says that it's "just sex," but God says that sex is a holy union between husband and wife. There is no "little sin" with God. The Bible says, "For whoever keeps the whole law and yet stumbles at just one point is guilty of breaking all of it" (James 2:10).

In a 2000 CNN poll concerning the Ten Commandments, 64 percent of Americans said that they would steal if they knew they could get away with it. Seventy-four percent of Americans said that they would lie under certain circumstances. What do our children see in our lives to help them choose how to live? College freshmen who encounter challenges to their spiritual heritage must be prepared to answer, "How will I live?"

If we are in a job where we are required to do unethical and dishonest things, we are going to have to make a choice. The question is, "How am I going to live—according to my culture or according to what's right?" Again, falling into some horrible sin is not our greatest temptation. Our greatest temptation is to compromise our convictions gradually so that we eventually become like everybody else.

YOUR GREATEST TRIUMPH

The greatest triumph in life is to stay pure in the midst of moral decay. "But Daniel resolved not to defile himself with the royal food and wine" (Dan. 1:8). When I was a teenager, I read a booklet titled "Dare to Be a Daniel." I don't remember many of the details, but I recall that Daniel dared to be different. Likewise, we must dare to stand up in the face of our godless culture and say, "I will not defile myself. I won't go along with the crowd. I'm willing to be different."

If we make the same choice as Daniel, we'll find that it is a *hard decision*. Peer pressure will try to force us to go along with the crowd. We will also find that it is a *humble decision*. Daniel requested humbly that he not defile himself. He didn't make a big deal about it. He wasn't judgmental, demanding that everyone else follow his diet too. When we dare to be a Daniel, our choice will also be an honored decision.

God says, "Those who honor Me I will honor" (1 Sam. 2:30 NASB). We see the results of Daniel's decision right away. After ten days of eating *zeroim* (fruit, vegetables, and grain), Daniel and his friends looked wonderful. They were handsome, strong, and healthy. Later, the king invited Daniel into his courts, and he became an influential dream interpreter for the king. We'll study later how this role put him under even more pressure, yet he continued to rely on his principled plan.

THE DANIEL DIET

The word *diet* originally meant more than the food one consumed; it described an individual's way of life, encompassing his or her emotional, spiritual, social, and physical dimensions. However, we've since reduced the idea of a diet to high fat, low carbs (or is it high carbs, low fat?) or the latest herbal concoction. In our results-oriented society, diet fads impress us. We want to know just enough about "busting" sugar and Atkins's latest findings to add a comment or two around the office water cooler.

Daniel followed a physical diet, but more importantly, he practiced the original meaning of the word—a godly way of life that encompassed his whole person. The most important lesson about Daniel isn't his food plan; it is his willingness to follow God's plan.

Without following a prayerfully constructed plan, Daniel would have failed the temptations and trials that came his way. He wasn't so "together" that a knee-jerk response to temptation would suffice. No, he had to prepare for the trial beforehand—just as we must do. He determined his steps in advance, committing to obey God in every way. *His* plan was *God's* plan for him.

A crisis of character is when everything around us is on the brink of chaos and the trials and temptations seem more than we can bear. We find ourselves out of options. We've tried our own plans and schemes and been left wanting. We realize we can't get it done on our own. In that moment, each of us must recognize that God alone has the best plan for our life—one that navigates us through the trials and problems and promises to shape us into His image without compromise.

For Daniel, this lesson at the king's table was only the first step in God's plan for him. God's plan for success starts with our commitment to a new *diata*, meaning a new "manner of living." Naturally, the first day of any diet is the most difficult. But it doesn't end there for us, and it didn't end there for Daniel. Daniel's enemies pursued him and his friends relentlessly. Ultimately, they tossed him into a pit of ravenous lions. However, we know that God shut the mouths of the lions and kept him safe. Yet, if Daniel had not initially "shut his mouth" to the king's food and wine, how do we know that God would have shut the mouths of the lions later in his life? If there had been no story of Daniel in the dining room, maybe there would have been no story of Daniel in the lion's den, or perhaps it would have been a very short story . . . with Daniel as the main character *and* the main dish!

Are we ready to go on to the other life lessons Daniel has for us? Or will we stop now, decide that it's too difficult, and settle for a short story instead?

Chapter Two

Performing Under Pressure

In the second year of his reign, Nebuchadnezzar had dreams; his mind was troubled and he could not sleep. So the king summoned the magicians, enchanters, sorcerers and astrologers to tell him what he had dreamed. When they came in and stood before the king, he said to them, "I have had a dream that troubles me and I want to know what it means." Then the astrologers answered the king in Aramaic, "O king, live forever! Tell your servants the dream, and we will interpret it." The king replied to the astrologers, "This is what I have firmly decided: If you do not tell me what my dream was and interpret it, I will have you cut into pieces and your houses turned into piles of rubble. But if you tell me the dream and explain it, you will receive from me gifts and rewards and great honor. So tell me the dream and interpret it for me.

—Daniel 2:1–6

On the morning of April 14, 1865, President Abraham Lincoln gathered with his cabinet at the White House in Washington as the bloody Civil War was ending. Unusually distracted during their discussion, Abraham Lincoln's thoughts digressed. He told his cabinet members that he had been having a strange dream the last few nights. As his bewildered cabinet members listened, the president went on to describe the details of his dream. In it, he saw a ship, and it was sailing towards some indefinite shore. He kept having that dream but didn't understand what it meant. The elusive meaning, however, would become all too clear later that night as President and Mrs. Lincoln attended a show at Ford's theater, and John Wilkes Booth shot him in the back of the head, inflicting a mortal wound. The next day, the "ship" that was the life of Abraham Lincoln reached the shore of eternity. Who could have guessed the personal, national, and eternal significance of Lincoln's dream?

In this chapter, we'll consider another national leader's dream from twenty-six hundred years ago that also had personal, national, and eternal significance. In Daniel 2:1, we learn that King Nebuchadnezzar was having a bout with insomnia. That Babylonian king, one of the greatest world leaders of the time, was the first person to conquer the entire civilized world—from what we would today call Italy all the way to Egypt. He built the beautiful ancient city of Babylon, located forty miles from modern Baghdad, Iraq. In fact, Saddam Hussein actually declared himself the reincarnation of Nebuchadnezzar. Before the Gulf War, Hussein claimed that he would rebuild ancient Babylon and restore the city to its former status as a world power. However, history tells us that Nebuchadnezzar's desire for worldly success led to his demise—as Hussein discovered during the second war between Iraq and the United States-led coalition in 2003. We'll study Nebuchadnezzar's downfall in another chapter. Let's pick up the story of Nebuchadnezzar's troubled sleep.

> So the king summoned the magicians, enchanters, sorcerers and astrologers to tell him what he had dreamed. When they came

in and stood before the king, he said to them, "I have had a dream that troubles me and I want to know what it means." Then the astrologers answered the king in Aramaic, "O king, live forever! [That's how his court always addressed the king.] Tell your servants the dream, and we will interpret it." (Dan. 2:2–4)

Now, who were those guys? They were the king's wise men—practicing sorcerers and astrologers—who advised the king in important business matters. They were the original "code breakers" because the Babylonians used codebooks to decipher the meaning of certain dreams. All the king had to say was, "This is what I dreamed," and these so-called wise men would get together, consult their codebooks, and offer an interpretation.

Yet, this particular dream was about to become the code breakers' worst nightmare. The problem began in verse 5: "The king replied to the astrologers, 'This is what I have firmly decided: If you do not tell me what my dream was and interpret it . . .'" In other words, he refused to tell them the details of the dream first. He wanted to test their abilities. "You're the psychics. You tell me what the dream was and interpret it." In fact, the king raised the stakes a little higher. Their penalty, if they couldn't tell him the dream and interpret it, is found in verses 5 and 6: "I will have you cut into pieces and your houses turned into piles of rubble. But if you tell me the dream and explain it, you will receive from me gifts and rewards and great honor. So tell me the dream and interpret it for me."

Perhaps Nebuchadnezzar suspected that these self-proclaimed experts were phonies. Maybe he thought, *I'm going to put these guys to the test and see if they can really perform the supernatural.* Even today, it's not uncommon for business leaders to rely on the same questionable tactics for their decision making. According to one study, more than two hundred of the Fortune 500 companies have at one time or another consulted an astrologer about the best time to do business.

I once heard former First Lady Barbara Bush tell the story about an astrologer who gave an unsolicited reading for her in 1984. This particular astrologer said that she and George Bush Sr. should never have married because they're both Geminis, and Geminis "don't get along" with other Geminis. As she finished telling the story, Mrs. Bush smiled and said, "You know, we've just celebrated fifty years of marriage. Every time I have a bad day, I tell George that astrologer was right."

Nebuchadnezzar's wise men were running out of options. "Once more they replied, 'Let the king tell his servants the dream, and we will interpret it'" (Dan. 2:7). However, the king wasn't going to fall for it.

> Then the king answered, "I am certain that you are trying to gain time, because you realize that this is what I have firmly decided: If you do not tell me the dream, there is just one penalty for you. You have conspired to tell me misleading and wicked things, hoping the situation will change. So then, tell me the dream, and I will know that you can interpret it for me." The astrologers answered the king, "There is not a man on earth who can do what the king asks!" (Dan. 2:8–10)

At least they were right about that. No human being *could* do it. In human terms, it was impossible. In fact, they went on to say, "No king, however great and mighty, has ever asked such a thing of any magician or enchanter or astrologer" (2:10). These guys were insulted; such a request wasn't in their job description! "What the king asks is too difficult. No one can reveal it to the king except the gods [small *g*], and they do not live among men" (2:11).

In the Babylonian culture, the people worshiped many gods (polytheism). Their gods were just impersonal forces; they had no personal relationship with the people. However, before long, those within the king's court would encounter a man who claimed a personal relationship with his God.

DANIEL UNDER PRESSURE

At this point, the king grew tired of their insinuations and excuses. Verse 12 says, "This made the king so angry and furious that he ordered the execution of all the wise men of Babylon." So he issued the decree to put these and all of the other wise men to death. Daniel and his three teenage friends were part of that group of wise men—all graduates of the king's college. When the king's commander set out to obey the decree, Daniel was at the top of the list. Let's discover how Daniel performed under mounting pressure, beginning with an encounter with the king's high court.

Facing Impossible Demands

When the king asked the wise men to read his mind, the wise men said, "That's impossible." And it was—even for Daniel, who would soon be in their shoes. However, God specializes in the impossible.

Like Daniel, we will repeatedly face similar impossible demands in life, things that are humanly impossible. They won't necessarily be mysterious dreams; they'll involve marriages, finances, health crises, and relationships. From a *human* perspective, the solution is impossible. Yet, Jesus said in Mark 10:27, "With man this is impossible, but not with God; all things are possible with God."

All things *are possible* with God. Do we believe that? If we do, every time we encounter the impossible, we'll say, "That is an opportunity for God to do something humanly impossible." A number of years ago, in fact, I took an Exacto knife and literally cut the word *impossible* out of my dictionary so I wouldn't even know what the word meant. Now if someone were to ask me about the implications of cutting the word *impossible* out of my dictionary, I can't say. *Implication* was on the other side of *impossible,* and I had cut it out, too! However, I do know that all things are possible with God. That's the first thing we learn from Daniel under pressure.

The Importance of Using Wisdom and Tact

When the commander, sword in hand, showed up at Daniel's door, Daniel demonstrated his wisdom. "When Arioch, the commander of the king's guard, had gone out to put to death the wise men of Babylon, Daniel spoke to him with wisdom and tact" (Dan. 2:14). Daniel didn't lose his temper. He employed wisdom and tact. Imagine that a supervisor, pink slip in hand, came to someone's office door to fire that person for an unjust cause. Would the typical person in that unfair situation speak with wisdom and tact? Do we know the difference between the two terms? Wisdom is the ability to say the right thing; tact is the ability to say it the right way.

We need wisdom and tact in situations that test our composure. We might have the right information in a stressful situation, but the way we approach the situation is the key. "He asked the king's officer, 'Why did the king issue such a harsh decree?' Arioch then explained the matter to Daniel" (Dan. 2:15). Sometimes, under great pressure at work or at home, we "crack" and say things that we will later regret. Daniel's cool composure, however, thwarted a potentially life-threatening situation, and he was able to prepare his next move.

Difficult Situations Force Us to Rely on God Alone

Armed with the commander's explanation of all that had oc-curred in the king's presence earlier that day, Daniel began piec-ing together a strategy. His strategy forced him to rely on God alone.

> At this, Daniel went in to the king and asked for time, so that he might interpret the dream for him. Then Daniel returned to his house and explained the matter to his friends, Hananiah, Mishael and Azariah. He urged them to plead for mercy from the God of heaven concerning this mystery, so that he and his friends might not be executed with the rest of the wise men of Babylon. (Dan. 2:16–18)

Daniel's situation encourages us to examine the myth that many Christians believe when it comes to experiencing trials: "God will never put more on us than we can bear." I can almost hear some-one coming to poor Daniel right about then and saying, "Well, you're in a pretty tough spot there, Daniel, but God will never put more on you than you can bear." In difficult situations, we unfor-tunately often turn to terrible theology for some comfort. Actu-ally, the Bible teaches that God *will* sometimes allow us to carry a burden that is too heavy for us to bear. When we come to the point that we can't bear it any longer, we will finally trust God instead of trusting ourselves. Daniel purposefully positioned him-self into complete vulnerability and dependence upon God. As long as he believed that he could handle the problem by himself, he would not turn to God. Realizing the depths of our desperate situations motivates us to depend utterly and totally on God.

The apostle Paul never claimed that God wouldn't put more on us than we could bear. He wrote, "We were under great pressure, far beyond our ability to endure, so that we despaired even of life. Indeed, in our hearts we felt the sentence of death. But this happened that we might not rely on ourselves but on God, who raises the dead. He has delivered us from such a deadly peril, and he will deliver us. On him we have set our hope that he will continue to deliver us" (2 Cor. 1:8–10). When Daniel faced this impossibility, he couldn't say, "Well, I can handle it. I'll just tough it out." No, his situation forced him to turn to God and depend on Him.

USING A PRAYER STRATEGY

Daniel's first expression of his dependence on God was to pray and to plead with others involved to seek God in prayer. Prayer preceded any action that Daniel took on his own behalf. It was his first inclination.

When You Need Wisdom, Just Ask

When we face an unfair work situation in which our job is threatened, our human tendency might be to fire off a letter to Human Resources. Or in a family crisis, we might show up unannounced on a rebellious child's dorm room doorstep to get to the bottom of things. Without the foresight and temperance that prayer brings, we cannot hope to form an effective strategy to deal with our problems. We can hardly think straight in our anger or indignation, and that's no time to try to force the issue.

Prayer should be our first line of defense, not a last resort. We often approach our problems with a "solve it" mentality. We try to evaluate, investigate, mitigate, and solve it first. Then, when we can't solve it, we concede, "I guess I'd better pray about it." However, the Bible teaches the opposite strategy. "If any of you lacks wisdom, he should ask God, who gives generously to all without finding fault, and it will be given to him" (James 1:5). As soon as we face a problem, we must pray for God to give us wisdom to know what to do.

Pray Specifically

Daniel's strategy involved specific requests. He said, "God, I need to know the king's dream." Sometimes we pray so generally that it would be hard to know if God answered our prayer! Daniel needed a specific answer, and he prayed a specific prayer. Could it be that we are not receiving answers to our prayers because we are asking in general terms rather than making specific requests?

Pray Persistently

Years ago, I learned a great acrostic for prayer: P.U.S.H. Pray Until Something Happens! Daniel prayed and kept on praying. His prayers gave new meaning to the word *deadline*—he could not stop because the king's guards were waiting to execute him if God did not come through for him. Have our prayers ever raced the clock? Our problem might be that we stop praying too soon. Pray persistently.

Prayer and Praise

Because of Daniel's prayerful composure, God communicated the meaning of the king's dream in a vision that night. Convinced that the message was from God, Daniel praised Him. "I thank and praise you, O God of my fathers: You have given me wisdom and power, you have made known to me what we asked of you, you have made known to us the dream of the king" (Dan. 2:23).

Although he could not validate this message until he stood before Nebuchadnezzar and revealed his dream, Daniel claimed that God had answered his prayer. That's faith! In other words, he praised God for assuring him that He would answer his prayer. Daniel teaches us that the best time to thank God for the answer to our requests is right after we ask Him. We can't wait until we have the visible evidence of answered prayer; we must go ahead and thank Him in advance. That kind of faith pleases God. The Bible says this about praying for wisdom: "But when he asks, he must believe and not doubt, because he who doubts is like a wave of the sea, blown and tossed by the wind. That man should not think he will receive anything from the Lord" (James 1:6–7).

Dr. Helen Roseveare, an African missionary, relates the story about a premature birth in her village. The mother died in childbirth, and the infant needed to be warmed immediately. However, she did not have an incubator, and the old hot water bottle was badly torn. Dr. Roseveare quickly gathered some of the children in that little village clinic and said, "Boys and girls, we need to pray and ask God to give us a hot water bottle or this little baby is going to die." And so they began to pray. One girl prayed this prayer aloud: "Dear God, please send a hot water bottle today. Tomorrow will be too late, because by then, the baby will be dead." Remembering that the little infant and her sister were now orphans, she added, "Dear Lord, please send a dolly for the baby's sister, so she won't be so lonely. Amen."

According to Dr. Roseveare's account, that afternoon a parcel arrived from England—a gift that a group of Christians had put together months earlier. When the doctor opened the parcel, she discovered on the very top a hot water bottle. As Dr. Roseveare prepared the hot water bottle, the little girl who had prayed so specifically continued determinedly digging through the rest of the large parcel. "I know there's a doll in here," she mumbled as she searched the items. Sure enough, there at the bottom of the box was a little rag doll.

POSTURE UNDER PRESSURE

"Then Daniel went to Arioch, whom the king had appointed to execute the wise men of Babylon, and said to him, 'Do not execute the wise men of Babylon'" (Dan. 2:24). This would have been a great opportunity for Daniel to get rid of his rivals. He could easily have advised the commander to kill everyone else except him and his friends. Good politicians always strategize to eliminate the opposition. But that was not Daniel's way. These same wise men would cause him all kinds of trouble in the years to come. However, Daniel demonstrated grace and focused on the main task at hand—accompanying Arioch to see the king to interpret his dream and stop the bloodshed.

> The king asked Daniel (also called Belteshazzar), "Are you able to tell me what I saw in my dream and interpret it?" Daniel replied, "No wise man, enchanter, magician or diviner can explain to the king the mystery he has asked about, but there is a God in heaven who reveals mysteries. He has shown King Nebuchadnezzar what will happen in days to come. Your dream and the visions that passed through your mind as you lay on your bed are these: As you were lying there, O king, your mind turned to things to come, and the revealer of mysteries showed you what is going to happen. As for me, this mystery has been revealed to me, not because I have greater wisdom than other living men, but so that you, O king, may know the interpretation and that you may understand what went through your mind." (Dan. 2:26–30)

What a pressure-packed situation! Picture this—a teenager, standing before the most powerful man on earth with one shot to get it right or face certain death. That was Daniel's unenviable position as he strode into the king's high court. Yet we learn several things from his posture during pressure.

- Note that he did not bow down before the king and say, "Live forever, O king," the usual pagan form of address. He did not follow a "When in Babylon do as the Babylonians do" philosophy. He simply said, "I've got the answer to your problem." *When we kneel before God in prayer, we can stand before any authority with confidence.* When we've been in the audience of the King of Kings and the Lord of Lords, no other person intimidates us.
- He kept the focus off the king, but he also kept the focus off himself. He made clear that *God* interpreted the dream. He did not credit his own ability. After Daniel told the dream and interpreted it, we read, "Then King Nebuchadnezzar fell prostrate before Daniel and paid him honor and ordered that an offering and incense be presented to him. The king said to Daniel, 'Surely your God is the God of gods and the Lord of kings and a revealer of mysteries, for you were able to reveal this mystery'" (Dan. 2:46–47). Daniel stood up under the pressure. He sought God in prayer and depended on God's wisdom. As a result, even a pagan king acknowledged Daniel's God above all gods.

GOD IS ABLE TO DELIVER

Whatever pressure-filled situation you face, remember Daniel's theme: *There is a God in heaven, and He is able to deliver us.* When we admit, "I am unable," God says, "Yes, but I am able." Paul reminds us, "Now to him who is able to do immeasurably more than all we ask or imagine, according to his power that is at work within us, to him be glory in the church and in Christ Jesus throughout all generations, for ever and ever!" (Eph. 3:20–21).

Chapter Three

Keeping Your Cool When the Heat Is On

King Nebuchadnezzar made an image of gold, ninety feet high and nine feet wide, and set it up on the plain of Dura in the province of Babylon. He then summoned the satraps, prefects, governors, advisers, treasurers, judges, magistrates and all the other provincial officials to come to the dedication of the image he had set up. So the satraps, prefects, governors, advisers, treasurers, judges, magistrates and all the other provincial officials assembled for the dedication of the image that King Nebuchadnezzar had set up, and they stood before it. Then the herald loudly proclaimed, "This is what you are commanded to do, O peoples, nations and men of every language: As soon as you hear the sound of the horn, flute, zither, lyre, harp, pipes and all kinds of music, you must fall down and worship the image of gold that King Nebuchadnezzar has set up. Whoever does not fall down and worship will immediately be thrown into a blazing furnace."

—Daniel 3:1–6

Picture a massive plain with a huge, golden statue shimmering in the sunlight. Thousands of VIPs from the empire have gathered for this important occasion and are milling around in their Brooks Brothers suits waiting for things to start, a reporter from *Good Morning Babylon* makes his interview rounds amid an air of excitement and expectation.

Suddenly, the press secretary for the king calls for everyone's attention. A little man with a large ego, he nervously clears his throat, straightens his tie, and launches into his spiel.

"Okay, folks. Gather around, gather around. As you know, this is a really important day for all of us in Babylon."

"Louder! We can't hear you!" someone shouts from the back.

"*A-hem!* I *said* King Nebuchadnezzar is really glad you can be here today," he begins again, this time straining his piercing nasal tone.

The *Good Morning Babylon* reporter breaks in about that time in a hushed tone. "If you're just joining us this morning, we're reporting live from Babylon, where the king has recently completed construction on a golden idol of mammoth proportions. We're waiting for a cue from the king's orchestra assembled behind me here. We're told that at that time the king will issue the command for every official present today to simultaneously bow down to the image and pay their respect to King—"

The reporter suddenly starts adjusting his earpiece and seems to be listening intently.

"What's that? If they don't bow . . . what?"

"Sorry, folks. We seem to be having a bit of trouble with our signal. If I understand correctly, it seems that the king's men have just fired up the old smelting furnace behind the king's residence. Let's go now to Andrea reporting to us live from the scene of the furnace."

The camera pans in on a distressed reporter who is wiping her brow with her scarf and trying to keep her hair in place despite the blasts of hot air from the nearby furnace.

"I can confirm that the king has indeed fired up his furnace, and sources tell us that he has just issued an order for any official who refuses to bow to the golden image to be, er . . . well . . . toast. Back to you, Don."

"Thank you, Andrea. Looks like we're ready to go any minute now."

Suddenly, the orchestra begins to tune as the conductor raises his baton for the downbeat.

Now I don't know what song they played to get people to make a decision. There is an old Baptist invitation hymn titled "Almost Persuaded." Maybe the Babylonian symphony played "Almost Cremated" or "The Heat Is On." When the music began, there was a loud "whump!" as thousands of knees hit the dirt followed by a thunderous "whap!" as thousands of foreheads hit the ground A cloud of dust arose from the sudden motion, and when it cleared, all across the plain thousands of VIPs were bowing prostrate before the image—all except for three solitary figures, three Hebrew teenagers, arms crossed and their faces turned toward heaven.

SHADRACH, MESHACH, AND ABEDNEGO

Where was Daniel? Obviously, he wasn't there because we know that he wouldn't have bowed either. As a high-ranking member of the king's court, he likely was away on official business. These three young men would have to put into practice what they had learned from being in Daniel's presence. This time, he could not be with them.

To succeed, we must surround ourselves with people who are dedicated to the same principles and goals in life as we are. However, we can't always count on our mentors to be there during a time of testing. There comes a time when we must be strong on our own. When we are persecuted for our principles, we discover how strong (or weak) we really are. That was the situation facing Daniel's three Hebrew friends. Let's see how they fared.

THEY WOULD NOT BOW—THAT'S DEVOTION

This ninety-foot-tall statue was just one of the many building projects that Nebuchadnezzar pursued to promote his own greatness. To give you perspective, the Statue of Liberty in New York Harbor is 130 feet from head to toe. This statue, built twenty-six centuries earlier, was almost as tall! Nebuchadnezzar had the statue built to glorify himself, although Daniel had informed him earlier that he served as king only because the God of heaven had placed him on the throne. We will study how Nebuchadnezzar got a rude reminder of God's authority later in another chapter.

The Septuagint (the Greek translation of the Old Testament) tells us that the statue was crafted in a man's image. It represented the best of industrial and scientific technology of that day. Do you recall the story of the Tower of Babel in Genesis 11? It was a human attempt to build a stairway to heaven—humanity's own way to God. In response, God confused the people's speech so they could no longer understand each other to finish the project. Babel eventually became known as the city of Babylon. Many archeologists contend that Nebuchadnezzar's statue was built in the exact same location as the tower from centuries earlier.

Both the Tower of Babel and Nebuchadnezzar's statue represent a philosophy called *humanism*, which enthrones man above God. The unofficial national religion of today's America is humanism, and millions of people bow to it every day. This philosophy has found its way into the workplace, the community, and many public schools.

1. Humanists regard the universe as self-existing and not created.
2. Man is a part of nature, and he has emerged as a result of a continuous process.

3. Traditional dogmatic or authoritarian religions that place revelation, God, ritual, or creed above human needs and experience do a disservice to the human species.
4. We affirm that moral values derive their source from human experience.
5. Intolerant attitudes, often cultivated by orthodox religions and puritanical cultures, unduly repress sexual conduct . . . short of harming others or compelling them to do likewise, individuals should be permitted to express their sexual proclivities and pursue their lifestyle as they desire.[1]

The preceding is excerpted from the *Humanist Manifesto II* published in 1973. Sound familiar? Sadly, millions of Americans today are worshiping at the altar of humanism. It's the most popular religion in America. Fortunately, three young men in this story refused to offer their devotion to humanism. They reserved their allegiance for God alone.

THEY WOULD NOT BEND—THAT'S DETERMINATION

Furious with rage, Nebuchadnezzar summoned Shadrach, Meshach and Abednego. So these men were brought before the king, and Nebuchadnezzar said to them, "Is it true, Shadrach, Meshach and Abednego, that you do not serve my gods or worship the image of gold I have set up? Now when you hear the sound of the horn, flute, zither, lyre, harp, pipes and all kinds of music, if you are ready to fall down and worship the image I made, very good. [He gave them a second chance to bow.] But if you do not worship it, you will be thrown immediately into a blazing furnace. Then what god will be able to rescue you from my hand?" (Dan. 3:13–15)

Nebuchadnezzar raised a good question when he gave them a second chance to bow before the golden image: Who could possibly save them if they were tossed into the fire? It's a question we need to address today. What God (or god) will be able to rescue you from trouble? The god of the Koran? The god of the New Age Religion? Or the God of the Bible? If you answer that question correctly, you can face any problem with confidence. These three boys had to have faith in someone reliable to respond the way they did. Consider their confident reply to the most powerful man on earth:

> Shadrach, Meshach and Abednego replied to the king, "O, Nebuchadnezzar, we do not need to defend ourselves before you in this matter [in other words, "We don't need to think about what to say; our minds are already made up"]. If we are thrown into the blazing furnace, the God we serve is able to save us from it, and he will rescue us from your hand, O king. But even if he does not, we want you to know, O king, that we will not serve your gods or worship the image of gold you have set up." (Dan. 3:16–18)

When Nebuchadnezzar summoned them to give them a second chance, he shrewdly called them by their Babylonian names (their Jewish names were Hananiah, Mishael, and Azariah). He used every trick to intimidate them into losing their determination. He had changed both their names and their addresses when he geographically uprooted them; however, he couldn't change their allegiance to the God of the Bible. The world will give us plenty of opportunities to renounce our commitments. The Bible says that the world is on a wide and welcoming road—the road to destruction. However, Jesus says that we must be determined to find the narrow path leading to life—and stay on it (Matt. 7:13–14).

THEY WOULD NOT BURN—THAT'S DELIVERANCE

Then Nebuchadnezzar was furious with Shadrach, Meshach
and Abednego, and his attitude toward them changed. He ordered the furnace heated seven times hotter than usual and
commanded some of the strongest soldiers in his army to tie
up Shadrach, Meshach and Abednego and throw them into
the blazing furnace. So these men, wearing their robes, trou-
sers, turbans and other clothes, were bound and thrown into
the blazing furnace. The king's command was so urgent and
the furnace was so hot that the flames of the fire killed the
soldiers who took up Shadrach, Meshach and Abednego, and
these three men, firmly tied, fell into the blazing furnace. (Dan.
3:19–23)

Biblical archeologists suggest that this was a brick furnace
shaped like an old milk bottle, wider at the bottom with an opening through which metals could be inserted to heat them during
the smelting process. Then there would be an opening somewhere
halfway up where fuel could be added to the fire by the king's
workers, who stood on some kind of scaffold. Finally, there was
also a narrow opening at the top to allow the smoke to escape.

After the response of the three Hebrews, the king was so furious that *he* was the one burning. He ordered the furnace to be
superheated. The only way to get a fire hotter is to introduce more
oxygen, so they probably had some kind of bellows that started
pumping more air into the fire. The sparks were flying, the flames
were roaring, and the smoke was billowing out of the top.

The fire was so hot that the soldiers who dragged the young
men up the scaffolding succumbed to the heat. They died just as
they dropped the three boys into the fire.

Then King Nebuchadnezzar leaped to his feet in amazement and asked his advisers, "Weren't there three men that we tied up and threw into the fire?" They replied, "Certainly, O king." He said, "Look! I see four men walking around in the fire, unbound and unharmed, and the fourth looks like a son of the gods." Nebuchadnezzar then approached the opening of the blazing furnace and shouted, "Shadrach, Meshach and Abednego, servants of the Most High God, come out! Come here!" So Shadrach, Meshach and Abednego came out of the fire, and the satraps, prefects, governors and royal advisers crowded around them. They saw that the fire had not harmed their bodies, nor was a hair of their heads singed; their robes were not scorched, and there was no smell of fire on them. (Dan. 3:24–27)

Nebuchadnezzar was amazed because he saw *four* men walking around in the fire Nebuchadnezzar observed in his pagan language, "The fourth one looks like a son of the gods." In verse 28, he even called the fourth man an angel. Who was the fourth man?

The majority of Jewish scholars have identified this person as an angel. The Talmud asserts that it was the angel Gabriel. However, the expression "a son of the gods" ascribes deity to the being, since an offspring of the gods partakes of the divine nature. The King believed he saw no less than a God in the flames with the Hebrews. From a Christian perspective, we know that the preincarnate Christ did appear to individuals in the Old Testament. Most likely the fourth man in the fire was the Lord God Himself, in the person of His son, the Lord Jesus Christ, who is sometimes called the Angel of the Lord.[2]

Without being dogmatic about his exact identity, we can say that the fourth person was God's man. I personally believe that it was one of the rare visits of Jesus to earth before Bethlehem—an Old Testament appearance of the Son of God coming down from heaven in bodily form. He stood up from His heavenly throne, stepped across the battlements of heaven, walked down the starry staircase, walked into the blazing furnace, and said to the flames, "Cool it!" And they did. And He was waiting for Shadrach, Meshach, and Abednego in the fire and said, "Chill, guys." And they did. The ropes around their hands and feet were incinerated, yet their flesh was not burned. When Nebuchadnezzar called these three young men out of the furnace, he noted that their clothes didn't smell like smoke nor was their hair burned. God had delivered them. What a miracle!

Some so-called "enlightened scholars" have tried to go through the Bible and remove the miracles and just make it a book of moral lessons. They claim that the story of Daniel's friends and the other miracles are intellectually inexplicable and, therefore, unacceptable. Because they cannot understand it, they reject it. However, the Bible says, "Trust in the Lord with all your heart and do not lean on your own understanding" (Prov. 3:5–6 NASB). So much of the Bible can't be explained reasonably and logically. The Bible is not irrational; it is suprarational. If you try to lean on your own understanding (and consequently stumble over the miracles of the Bible), you'll have a hard time knowing God. He is beyond human rationality.

A good definition of a miracle is "when Jesus shows up." We might find ourselves in deep trouble just as these three young men did—past the point of being able to rescue ourselves. We need Jesus to show up in a mighty way. If we continue thrashing about in our own independence, refusing to rely on God to deliver us, we may be missing our miracle. We may feel too guilty to ask for help because we are in moral trouble. Our own ego may get in the way when we are in financial trouble. We desperately need Jesus to show up and walk with us, but we won't ask for help. How sad. The only way to keep from getting burned when the heat is on is to seek and submit to God's deliverance.

LIFE LESSONS LEARNED FROM THE FURNACE

Persecution: Facing the Fire Deepens Your Commitment

Persecution comes whenever we dare to be like Daniel and his friends and refuse to bow down to the idols of this world. Second Timothy 3:12 says, "In fact, everyone who wants to live a godly life in Christ Jesus *will* be persecuted" (emphasis added). Have you discovered that sold-out Christians bug the average American? A Sunday-only Christian seems to fit into society just fine, but once you decide to be a 24/7 Christian, you are deemed a religious fanatic. If you are at work and somebody tells a filthy joke but you don't laugh, how does everyone react? They will look at you as though you were weird. When you exercise the nerve to politely ask that someone please not use your Savior's name as profanity, you are considered a kook! If you're living a godly life, some people won't like you. In fact, if you are not experiencing some level of persecution, it could be that your life is so worldly and so ungodly that you don't qualify for it!

Persecution actually serves a purpose in our lives when we allow God to use it to make us stronger. Do you think the boys at the beginning of this story had any idea how strongly they believed their convictions? Without the furnace, they might have been content to live in the shadow of Daniel—their leader—and never have known God's power. Untested convictions are not really convictions at all; they're just strong opinions until the heat is on.

I've been through the fire a few times, and I expect I'll go through it again. Yet I've found that during the times of hottest persecution, I've been driven to my knees, and my intimacy with Jesus has deepened. For that reason, I wouldn't trade the fiery furnace experiences. Just think. If Shadrach, Meshach and Abednego hadn't been thrown into the fire, they wouldn't have had the chance to "walk" with Jesus.

Perseverance: Don't Give in to Peer Pressure

Like the boys in this story, you must determine *before* the crisis arises that you will be faithful. Don't wait for the "heat of the moment." If you haven't already decided to honor God, it's a tough choice to make with the heat of the furnace warming your face. For example, you must determine in a moment of quiet clarity to remain both sexually pure until marriage and monogamous after marriage. Don't wait until you're in a sexually charged situation to choose purity. You will generally lose. There is great power in a predetermined decision.

You must resist the temptation to want to be like everyone else. That's called peer pressure. How do you think our three friends felt when everyone else around them was bowing down? They felt different, out of place, strange. And no person, no matter how godly he or she is, likes the feeling of being different.

A few years ago, a major university worked with the old television show *Candid Camera* to conduct some psychological experiments on the power of peer pressure. It was scientific study, but it was also very entertaining. In one episode, they put actors in the waiting room of a doctor's office, and all of the actors were wearing only underwear. They wanted to see what unsuspecting patients would do when they walked in and saw everyone already undressed (after all, the doctor is going to tell you to take off your clothes anyway, right?). They were surprised that most of the unsuspecting patients walked in, signed the book, looked around, and, without a word, started taking off their clothes! That's the power of peer pressure.

In another experiment, they put actors on an elevator and had all of them face the back of the elevator instead of the door, just to see what people would do. Most of the unsuspecting people got on, pushed their button, and turned with the crowd to face the back of the elevator. That's peer pressure.

If you are going to dare to be a Daniel (or a Shadrach, Meshach, or Abednego) and stand up for what's right, you will often have to stand alone. Yes, it's sometimes painful to be faithful. You have to endure the scorn and the ridicule thrown your way, but remember that God will honor your endurance. First Peter 2:20 says, "But how is it to your credit if you receive a beating for doing wrong and endure it? But if you suffer for doing good and you endure it, this is commendable before God."

Presence: Jesus Will Be with You in the Fire

Now, let's do a little math lesson. How many men were thrown *into* the fire? Three. How many men walked around in the fire? Four. How many men walked *out* of the fire? Three. So where is the fourth man? He's still *in* the fire, and you'll find Him there when you have to walk through the fire yourself. Look at God's promise in Isaiah 43:2–4: "When you walk through the fire, you will not be burned; the flames will not set you ablaze. For I am the Lord, your God, the Holy One of Israel, your Savior. . . . Since you are precious and honored in my sight, and because I love you . . ."

Notice that it doesn't say that God will keep you out of the fire. And it doesn't say, "*If* you walk through the fire . . ." It says, "*When* you walk through the fire . . ." Although God didn't keep them from the fire, He did keep the fire from them!

Would you rather stay out of the fire and miss a walk with Jesus or go through the fire and walk *with* Jesus? I know your answer is, "I want to avoid the fire *and* walk with Jesus." Sometimes that's not possible because He is in the fire. He lived a life that got Him into trouble until He was crucified. Problems are going to come into our lives. We might lose our jobs or lose our homes. Some of us will go through the excruciating pain of losing a loved one through death or divorce. However, during these times of fiery trials, we find the strength and grace of Jesus in unique ways.

Purification: God Uses the Fire to Purify You

You might say, "I don't like the fire. I'm afraid of the fire. Why doesn't God just keep me out of the fire in the first place?" Or you might be facing a private, personal, painful furnace right now, and you want to know, "What is God doing? Why am I going through this fire?" Malachi 3:3 says, "He will sit as a refiner and purifier of silver; he will purify the Levites [priests] and refine them like gold and silver. Then the Lord will have men who will bring offerings in righteousness. . . ."

A silversmith places the silver in the crucible and heats the crucible until the silver becomes liquid. The liquid silver sinks to the bottom, and the impurities rise to the top. Then the silversmith skims off the impurities that dilute the silver's purity. He carefully regulates the heat so the silver is not damaged; it's just hot enough to remove the impurities.

God acts much like a silversmith. You and I are like the silver in the crucible—our own fiery trial. We wish He would turn the heat down. Do you know *how* the silversmith knows *when* the silver has become pure? It's when he can see a clear reflection of his own face in the surface of the molten silver. When the silver becomes like a mirror, he knows it's pure, and he removes the silver from the fire. God wants to see in us a reflection of His godly character.

I can imagine Jesus looking into the eyes of Shadrach, Meshach, and Abednego in the furnace. What did He see? He saw a reflection of the time when He Himself would endure the fire of the Cross for each of us. And when He saw that kind of unselfish nature, He said, "You boys can leave the fire now because you have been purified." When Jesus, the Silversmith, looks into your face, can He see His own nature reflected—love, joy, peace, patience, gentleness, goodness, meekness, faithfulness, and self-control? If that has not happened yet, thank Him for the fire that He is using to purify you, and continue to stay close to Jesus in the midst of the fire. The only way you can keep your cool when the heat is on is to look for Jesus in the fire and walk with Him.

Chapter Four

Surrendering Your Lifestyle

I, Nebuchadnezzar, was at home in my palace, contented and prosperous. I had a dream that made me afraid. As I was lying in my bed, the images and visions that passed through my mind terrified me. . . .

In the visions I saw while lying in my bed, I looked, and there before me was a messenger, a holy one, coming down from heaven. He called in a loud voice: "Cut down the tree and trim off its branches; strip off its leaves and scatter its fruit. Let the animals flee from under it and the birds from its branches. But let the stump and its roots, bound with iron and bronze, remain in the ground, in the grass of the field.

"Let him be drenched with the dew of heaven, and let him live with the animals among the plants of the earth. Let his mind be changed from that of a man and let him be given the mind of an animal, till seven times pass by for him."

—Daniel 4:4–5, 13–16

What would be your reaction if you turned on CNN one morning to learn that Saddam Hussein had become a Christian overnight through a prison ministry such as Prison

Fellowship? Imagine if he appeared in a press conference, donning a prison uniform, and announced, "I realized recently that for the past several years I have been out of my mind—I have been acting like a beast. However, the God of Israel has now opened my eyes. I have renounced Islam, and I am now trusting the God of Israel. I have given my heart to Jesus Christ, and I plan to spend the rest of my days serving Him."

His capture was a stunning moment—but this would be an astonishing event. Now, perhaps you can better imagine the surprise of the Babylonian people twenty-six hundred years ago when their pagan king (ruling the same territory as modern Iraq) announced a similar experience. In fact, Daniel 4 is all about King Nebuchadnezzar's conversion experience. This book within a book tells of the magnificent failures and dreadful successes of Daniel's contemporary world leader, Nebuchadnezzar. It's an exposé of what happens when the success of this world dissuades you from God's perfect plan for living. Let's relive this drama scene by scene.

SCENE ONE: A DREAM RECEIVED (4:4–18)

About thirty years had elapsed between chapter 3—the story of the fiery furnace—and Daniel chapter 4. Daniel is probably in his mid-fifties at the time, and Nebuchadnezzar is approaching seventy. The king begins his tale with a flashback—a frightening dream he had. (He had a lot of dreams!) This time, the king dreamed about a massive tree that was healthy and thriving. However, this tranquil dream quickly became a nightmare.

> In the visions I saw while lying in my bed, I looked, and there before me was a messenger, a holy one, coming down from heaven. He called in a loud voice: "Cut down the tree and trim off its branches; strip off its leaves and scatter its fruit. Let the

animals flee from under it and the birds from its branches. But let the stump and its roots, bound with iron and bronze, remain in the ground, in the grass of the field. Let him be drenched with the dew of heaven, and let him live with the animals among the plants of the earth. Let his mind be changed from that of a man and let him be given the mind of an animal, till seven times pass by for him." (Dan. 4:13–16)

Anxious to know what this dream might mean for himself and the future of his kingdom, Nebuchadnezzar sent for his wise men—again. As before, the wise men were unable to interpret the dream. So the king sent for his star dream-revealer, Daniel.

SCENE TWO: A DREAM REVEALED (4:19–27)

Then Daniel (also called Belteshazzar) was greatly perplexed for a time, and his thoughts terrified him. So the king said, "Belteshazzar, do not let the dream or its meaning alarm you." Belteshazzar answered, "My lord, if only the dream applied to your enemies and its meaning to your adversaries! The tree you saw, which grew large and strong, with its top touching the sky, visible to the whole earth, with beautiful leaves and abundant fruit, providing food for all, giving shelter to the beasts of the field, and having nesting places in its branches for the birds of the air—you, O king, are that tree! You have become great and strong; your greatness has grown until it reaches the sky, and your dominion extends to distant parts of the earth." (Dan. 4:19–22)

Indeed, by human standards, Nebuchadnezzar was one of the greatest kings in history. However, the king could not bask in his greatness for long. In his dream, an angel took a heavenly chain saw, cranked it, revved it up a few times, and proceeded to cut down the tree. Timber! Nebuchadnezzar would fall from the height of greatness. The bigger they are, the harder they fall.

Daniel continues:

> You will be driven away from people and will live with the wild animals; you will eat grass like cattle and be drenched with the dew of heaven. Seven times will pass by for you until you acknowledge that the Most High is sovereign over the kingdoms of men and gives them to anyone he wishes. The command to leave the stump of the tree with its roots means that your kingdom will be restored to you when you acknowledge that Heaven rules. Therefore, O king, be pleased to accept my advice: Renounce your sins by doing what is right, and your wickedness by being kind to the oppressed. It may be that then your prosperity will continue. (Dan. 4:25–27)

This disaster did not overtake Nebuchadnezzar overnight. Certainly, the dream troubled him, and Daniel's interpretation was frightening, but as the king pondered his predicament, his eyes fell on the grandeur of his throne room and the expanse of his kingdom. He concluded that he was simply too strong, too important, and too powerful for this to happen; he would fight it. He convinced himself that he would *never* fall.

What did the king see when he gazed over the city of Babylon? He looked with pride at his Hanging Gardens, one of the Seven Wonders of the ancient world. He had built these massive gardens for his wife, Amytis. She came from Media, where there were mountains and vegetation, but Babylon was flat. So Nebuchadnezzar constructed an artificial mountain and planted gardens that hung down the side of this structure such that these gardens seemed to be growing in the air. He also devised an ingenious system to hoist water more than three hundred feet from the Euphrates River to water these gardens. He was a brilliant builder.

Babylonian records tell us that he had three massive palaces in the city. His main palace was 350 yards long and 200 yards wide (that's yards, not feet). Today, we think of a house as being palatial if it has 10,000 square feet. Nebuchadnezzar's main palace was 630,000 square feet. Although he was shaken by the dream, as he wandered the rooftops of his estate, he thought, *Look what I have done!*

Beyond Nebuchadnezzar's own royal grounds, the city of Babylon was an architectural marvel. Records indicate that two million people lived there, making it the largest city in the world at the time. A wide, one thousand-yard-long ceremonial boulevard (equivalent to ten football fields) ran down the center of the city. A double-wall system encircled the main city. Its inner wall was twenty-one feet thick and reinforced with defense towers at sixty-foot intervals. The outer wall was thirty-eight feet high and eleven feet wide and also had watchtowers. Later, Nebuchadnezzar added another defensive double-wall system. It ran for seventeen miles and was wide enough at the top for chariots to pass. As he considered his accomplishments, he was filled with pride.

The sin of pride is one of the toughest sins to detect because a person can be proud and not realize it. You're aware when you steal something. You know when you lie or commit adultery. But you can be guilty of pride and confuse it with "feeling good about yourself" or "having a positive self-image." Pride occurs when you start thinking that every good thing in your life is a result of who you are and what you have done. It removes God from the equation. First Peter 5:5 says, "God opposes the proud but gives grace to the humble."

It's a dangerous habit to stroll along the roof of your personal kingdom and start thinking about how great you are. You think that you are on top of the world and that you have everything under control. You feel as though you are the ruler of your own little kingdom. However, watch out! Proverbs 16:18 says, "Pride goes before destruction, a haughty spirit before a fall."

After Daniel's cautionary speech, one month passed . . . and nothing that Daniel had predicted happened. The king began to relax. Six months passed. Nothing. "I'm okay. Daniel was wrong," the king must have told himself. Eleven more months passed. "Ha! Why did I ever worry? I'm invincible, just as I thought."

A full year passed before Nebuchadnezzar's downfall occurred. Why do you think God waited an entire year? The answer is found in 2 Peter 3:9: "The Lord is not slow in keeping his promise, as some understand slowness. He is patient with you, not wanting anyone to perish, but everyone to come to repentance."

You might be like Nebuchadnezzar: you hear a message about repentance, and you get a little bothered and think, *You know, I really need to repent.* But then, after a week or a month passes, and everything seems to be "fine" in your life, you say, "Nah, everything is okay." A year may pass, forty years may pass, seventy years may pass, and everything is fine. Just remember: God's promises may seem slow in coming, but they are sure. Let's continue the story.

SCENE THREE: A DREAM REALIZED (4:28–33)

All this happened to King Nebuchadnezzar. Twelve months later, as the king was walking on the roof of the royal palace of Babylon, he said, "Is not this the great Babylon I have built as the royal residence, by my mighty power and for the glory of my majesty?" The words were still on his lips when a voice came from heaven, "This is what is decreed for you, King

Nebuchadnezzar: Your royal authority has been taken from you. You will be driven away from people and will live with the wild animals; you will eat grass like cattle. Seven times will pass by for you until you acknowledge that the Most High is sovereign over the kingdoms of men and gives them to anyone he wishes." Immediately what had been said about Nebuchadnezzar was fulfilled. He was driven away from people and ate grass like cattle. His body was drenched with the dew of heaven until his hair grew like the feathers of an eagle and his nails like the claws of a bird. (Dan. 4:28–33)

Notice the first person pronouns in verse 30: "Is not this the great Babylon *I* have built as the royal residence, by *my* mighty power and for the glory of *my* majesty?" He gorged himself on his own self-importance. If anyone needed to put his ego on a diet, it was Nebuchadnezzar. And God showed up to serve him an extra large helping of humble pie!

I started to name this chapter "From Beauty to Beast" or the "Birdman of Babylon." Scientifically, there is a documented psychological phenomenon called lycanthrope. It comes from the Greek word for "wolf," *lycos,* and the word for "man," *anthropos. Lycanthrope* means literally "wolf man," although today the term is used regardless of the type of animal the person believes he or she is. Lycanthrope is a form of insanity in which a person is convinced that he is an animal. In fact, this odd condition inspired the primitive werewolf superstition long before Hollywood made werewolf movies. As a kid, I enjoyed going to the movies to watch the old black-and-white horror pictures. I can still remember seeing Lon Cheney play a werewolf. A look would come over his face, and he'd start growing hair and claws, and right before your eyes he would change into an animal. I'd get to shaking so hard that I'd spill my popcorn! Nebuchadnezzar was the first documented case of a wolf man! For seven years, he lived like an animal.

Try to imagine the transformation that took place as Nebuchadnezzar, the majestic king, became a beast! He could no longer live with people; he lived outside in the fields with grazing animals. His diet probably was not just grass because this word also refers to vegetables and other herbs. At night, Nebuchadnezzar wouldn't come inside. He stayed in the open field, exposed to the elements of nature. So, in the mornings he would be "drenched with the dew from heaven." His hair became matted and coarse and looked like eagle feathers. His fingernails and toenails, never cut, became like claws. God didn't have to perform some miracle to turn Nebuchadnezzar into a beast. He simply removed the constraints from his heart, and Nebuchadnezzar's true, beastly nature manifested itself.

This story is a lot closer to home than you might realize. Open your daily newspaper and consider the violent crimes that are being committed today. You'll agree that many, if not all of us, have a monster living within us—a beast that wants to feed on our inherent sinful nature. Jeremiah 17:9 really is true: "The heart is deceitful above all things, and desperately wicked: who can know it?" (KJV).

Nebuchadnezzar represents a life out of control. He can't even follow the basic rules of personal hygiene and diet. Has that happened to you? Not lycanthrope, but do you look in the mirror and wonder, *What's happened to me? My life is out of control.* You might look just as pretty or as handsome as ever on the outside, but you realize that you're not as pretty on the inside as you once believed. Do you find that hateful, angry, and bitter things come out of your mouth? Has some ugly, depraved behavior become a part of your life? Perhaps you don't like what you see on the inside because it's beastly. Perhaps God is revealing the depth of your capacity for evil to remind you just how much you need Him in your life.

You might have placed your trust in God's Son, Jesus Christ, at some point in your life, but perhaps you've never learned to daily surrender your lifestyle. The inner beast is always there, nudging you toward sin. The Bible says, "But sin, seizing the opportunity . . . produced in me every kind of covetous desire. . . . When I want to do good, evil is right there with me. For in my inner being I delight in God's law; but I see another law at work in the members of my body, waging war against the law of my mind. . . . What a wretched man I am! Who will rescue me from this body of death?" (Rom. 7:8, 21–24.) This internal struggle is why we don't consistently dare to be a Daniel—our present lifestyle is in constant conflict with what it should be—a surrendered one.

When we are willing to let God use us, He transforms both the potential and present chaos in our lives into character. Paul found the same secret in Romans: "Who will rescue me from this body of death? Thanks be to God—through Jesus Christ our Lord!" (7:24–25). Jesus has delivered you from the monster within, so live like it!

Remember Nebuchadnezzar's dream? For seven full years, he lived as a beastly creature, but God wasn't through with him. The tree was cut down, but the stump and the roots remained. This fact represents every person's hope that God can transform a beast into a beautiful person. Now let's see what God can do for a person who lives like a beast.

SCENE FOUR: A CHANGED MAN (4:34–37)

This passage contains Nebuchadnezzar's personal description of his transformation. He writes in Daniel 4:34, "At the end of that time, I, Nebuchadnezzar, raised my eyes toward heaven, and my sanity was restored. Then I praised the Most High; I honored and glorified him who lives forever." Contrast the next verse to the "old" Nebuchadnezzar, who had proclaimed, "Look what I have done!" "His dominion is an eternal dominion; his kingdom endures from generation to generation. All the peoples of the earth are regarded as nothing. He does as he pleases with the powers of heaven and the peoples of the earth. No one can hold back his hand or say to him: 'What have you done?'" (Dan. 4:34–35).

In verse 37, we discover what Nebuchadnezzar had learned: "Now, I, Nebuchadnezzar, praise and exalt and glorify the King of heaven, because everything he does is right and all his ways are just. And those who walk in pride he is able to humble." It took him seven years in God's University of Affliction, but he finally graduated!

We must avoid the sin of pride because Daniel 4 shows us what can happen when we are so enamored with ourselves that we think that God's universe revolves around us. Nebuchadnezzar learned that God is able to humble those who walk in pride. This chapter was written about a changed man, a man who had entered into a personal relationship with the God of the universe. History tells us that Nebuchadnezzar died soon after this experience. Don't be surprised if someday you see Nebuchadnezzar in heaven because God can change a birdman into a believer; He can transform a savage into a saint; He can turn a wolf man into a witness for Him. Imagine what He can do for you!

LESSONS TO LEARN FROM THE BIRDMAN OF BABYLON

Worldly Success Never Satisfies

Nebuchadnezzar had wealth beyond description, but he couldn't get a good night's sleep. He controlled a vast kingdom, but he couldn't control his passions. As long as he could fill his waking hours with activities to occupy his mind, he was fine. But when he was all alone in his royal chamber, snuggled under the royal covers of the royal bed, he knew that something was wrong. This troubling dream tormented him and robbed him of rest.

Do you have the sense of restlessness? Outwardly you are "prosperous and contented," but there's a huge, aching hole in the center of your heart. As long as you stay busy during the day, you don't notice it; but in the wee hours of the morning, when sleep won't come, you have the nagging certainty that something is missing. The same God who changed Nebuchadnezzar is after you too. Francis Thompson has written "The Hound of Heaven," which describes how God's Spirit pursues you to change you.

> I fled Him, down the nights and down the days;
> I fled Him, down the arches of the years;
> I fled Him, down the labyrinthine ways
> Of my own mind; and in the mist of tears
> I hid from Him, and under running laughter.
> Up vistaed hopes I sped;
> And shot, precipitated,
> Adown Titanic glooms of chasmed fears,
> From those strong Feet that followed, followed after.
> But with unhurrying chase,
> And unperturbed pace,
> Deliberate speed, majestic instancy,
> They beat—and a Voice beat
> More instant than the Feet
> "All things betray thee, who betrayest Me."[1]

Have you found that your possessions don't satisfy you? Many men and women are reaching their fifties after climbing the ladder of success only to find that it is leaning against the wrong building. Bob Buford wrote *Halftime* to address this phenomenon. Buford contends that most Americans spend the first half of their careers working their fingers to the bone to find success, only to find that they aren't happy. A lot of tired people drag their injured egos into the locker room of introspection and discover that they want to spend the second half searching for significance, not success.[2] True significance is found only in a relationship with Jesus Christ.

God Employs a Variety of Methods to Get Your Attention

God used a dream to irritate Nebuchadnezzar. Then he sent Daniel to get his attention. Next, God allowed Nebuchadnezzar to hit rock bottom. Is God trying to tell you something? He might be using Daniel 4 to get your attention. I hope you are more attentive than Nebuchadnezzar; don't wait until you are at rock bottom to listen to Him!

One of the greatest abilities is the art of being able to hear God's voice in the midst of all of the noise of this world. A story I once heard clearly illustrates this. Back when the telegraph was the fastest method of long-distance communication, a young man applied for a job as a Morse code operator. When he arrived, he entered a large, busy office filled with noise and clatter, including the clicking of a telegraph in the background. A sign on the receptionist's counter instructed job applicants to fill out a form and wait until they were summoned to enter the inner office. The young man filled out his form and sat down with the seven other applicants in the waiting area.

After a few minutes, the young man stood up and walked right in to the inner office—without being summoned. Naturally the other applicants perked up, wondering what was going on. They muttered among themselves that he had no business entering the other office.

Within a few minutes, however, the boss escorted the young man out of the office and said to the other applicants, "Gentlemen, thank you very much for coming, but I've given the job to this fellow."

The other applicants grumbled to each other, and one spoke up. "Wait a minute. I don't understand. He was the last to come in, and we never even got a chance to be interviewed. Yet he got the job. That's not fair!"

The boss said, "In the past thirty minutes while you've been sitting here, the telegraph has been ticking out the following message in Morse code: 'If you understand this message, then come right in. The job is yours.' None of you heard it or understood it. This young man did. The job is his."

We live in a world that, like that office, is full of busyness and clatter. Many people are too distracted to hear the still, small voice of God. Are you "tuned in" to God's voice? God is always speaking, but are you listening? Some of you are listening, but many of you are so distracted by the cares of this world that you are not "tuned in" to His voice.

God Always Warns—and Allows Repentance—Before He Acts

Before you criticize God for turning Nebuchadnezzar into a wild animal, remember that God warned him twelve months earlier in a dream. Then He sent His messenger, Daniel, who told him to repent. A road leads to God's judgment, and many people are traveling down it at an alarming speed. But all along the road God has placed plenty of warning signs. Every cemetery and obituary is a warning that you'll face death, and God is giving you time to repent.

Nebuchadnezzar had been warned before, but nothing had happened. Little did he know that when Daniel stood there and said, "Renounce your sins and start living right" it was to be his last warning before God's judgment fell.

As you read these lines, God is warning you again, and chances are you've been warned before. He is telling you to change—and offering to help you do it (Phil. 2:13). Could this be God's last warning for you? Only God knows.

When You Look to God, He Will Restore You

Nebuchadnezzar's problem was pride. As long as he was looking down at all he had accomplished, he was in trouble. Then for seven years he walked around like an animal, on all fours. He *had* to look down. Our God is the God of the second, third, and fourth chances. After Nebuchadnezzar was humbled, he looked in the right direction; he looked up. He lifted his eyes to God. The psalmist says in Psalm 121:1–2, "I lift up my eyes to the hills—where does my help come from? My help comes from the LORD, the Maker of heaven and earth."

Nebuchadnezzar said, "I . . . raised my eyes toward heaven, and my sanity was restored" (4:34). If you are struggling with the beast within, and you are fighting to keep a grip on your sanity, you must lift your eyes to God. Quit looking at your problems; lift your eyes to the Problem Solver. Quit looking at your affliction; lift your eyes to the Answer! Quit looking at your suffering; lift your eyes to the Savior. That's what Nebuchadnezzar did. He looked up and saw God. He acknowledged God's power and said, "Everything he does is right and all his ways are just. And those who walk in pride he is able to humble" (4:37).

TOO IMPORTANT TO IGNORE

On the night of April 14, 1912, the "unsinkable" RMS *Titanic* surged across a calm sea. We all know that she sank after glancing off an iceberg. Records indicate that earlier that night, several warnings had been sent to tell the crew that they were heading toward disaster, but the messages were ignored! In fact, when a nearby ship sent an urgent message warning them that they were compromising their safety going into an ice field, the radio operators on the *Titanic* were talking to Cape Race about what time the chauffeurs were to meet arriving passengers at the dock and what menus were to be ready. Preoccupied with this trivia, the *Titanic*'s radioman responded to the warning with, "Shut up! I am talking to Cape Race. You are jamming my signals!" Like Nebuchadnezzar, they worshiped their own glory and ignored the warnings. Unspeakable destruction soon followed.

Some things are too important to ignore. Are you listening to God's warning today? How many warnings to repent do you think you have left? Nebuchadnezzar heard God and allowed Him to change his heart. The same king who threw Shadrach, Meshach, and Abednego into the fiery furnace in chapter 3 now praised the God of heaven. Only God can bring about such a change.

The Hanging Gardens of Babylon are gone; we can only read about their beauty. The amazing city of Babylon is now buried under the sands of Iraq. The only thing Nebuchadnezzar produced that remains today is his personal testimony found in Daniel 4. Now, twenty-six hundred years later, God is still using it to draw people to Himself. The only thing that will stand the test of time is your testimony of how Jesus has changed your life and your lifestyle. The good news is that God has the power to turn not only self-centered beauties into beasts but also a beast of a sinner into a beauty of a saint.

Chapter Five

The Lions in Daniel's Den

It pleased Darius to appoint 120 satraps to rule throughout the kingdom, with three administrators over them, one of whom was Daniel. The satraps were made accountable to them so that the king might not suffer loss. Now Daniel so distinguished himself among the administrators and the satraps by his exceptional qualities that the king planned to set him over the whole kingdom. At this, the administrators and the satraps tried to find grounds for charges against Daniel in his conduct of government affairs, but they were unable to do so. They could find no corruption in him, because he was trustworthy and neither corrupt nor negligent. Finally these men said, "We will never find any basis for charges against this man Daniel unless it has something to do with the law of his God."

So the administrators and the satraps went as a group to the king and said: "O King Darius, live forever! The royal administrators, prefects, satraps, advisers and governors have all agreed that the king should issue an edict and enforce the decree that anyone who prays to any god or man during the next thirty days, except to you, O king, shall be thrown into the lions' den."

—Daniel 6:1–7

If most people know any story from the book of Daniel, it is the wonderful story of Daniel in the lions' den. Most of us first heard this story as children in Sunday school or when our parents taught us Bible stories. We remember Daniel and his courage in the face of hungry lions. My editor asked me if the title to this chapter was a misprint. No, the focus of our study is on the lions in this story—the lions in Daniel's den. You'll soon understand what I mean.

CHANGE IN COMMAND

At this point in chapter 6 of Daniel, our hero had lived through several Babylonian administrations, including Nebuchadnezzar's and Belshazzar's. We pick up the story of Daniel during the rule of a non-Babylonian king, Darius. He was a Mede by descent, a ruler who murdered Belshazzar, overtook his throne, and established what historians call the Medo-Persian Empire.

Perhaps you know what it's like to go through a change of administration at your job. When a new supervisor comes in with new ideas and unfamiliar methods, it's a challenge to adjust, even if the innovations are good. A new boss often creates an atmosphere in which people start jockeying for position, fearing that their current job might be eliminated unless they prove themselves to be indispensable. They assume that this is their moment, and they might as well make the most of it.

Likewise, when Darius came to power, things began to change, and so did the attitudes of the people in power. They got edgy, nervous. Darius decentralized his staff structure and appointed one hundred twenty satraps, or administrators, to rule throughout the kingdom. Daniel, then in his eighties, brought to the table his experience and familiarity with the people. He so distinguished himself among the administrators and the satraps by his "exceptional qualities" that the king planned to set him over the whole kingdom. The king's other employees began to resent Daniel's star performance because he threatened their own job security. How could this guy, who certainly was not a Persian, become second in command?

Daniel's Public Display of Purity

The Bible records the reaction of his rivals: "At this, the administrators and the satraps tried to find grounds for charges against Daniel in his conduct of government affairs, but they were unable to do so. They could find no corruption in him, because he was trustworthy and neither corrupt nor negligent" (Dan. 6:4).

The Persian leaders were jealous of Daniel, and they plotted to discredit him, but his reputation was flawless; there was nothing to expose. His life was pure. His conscience was clean. He was beyond reproach. Verse 3 tells us that he possessed "exceptional qualities," also translated "an excellent spirit" or a "surpassing spirit." The phrase "excellent spirit" means that he had a positive, winsome attitude about life that carried over into the workplace. This is especially noteworthy because he was past retirement age. When some people get older they become grumpy old men or grouchy old women. The longer a person lives, the easier it is to become cynical and develop a sour attitude.

Since I was a young man, I've asked God never to let me lose my zeal and enthusiasm, to whatever age He allows me to live. The word *enthusiasm* comes from two Greek words, *en* and *theos*. *En* means "in," and *theos* means "God." So the more "in" God you are, the more enthusiastic you will be! In contrast to his peers, Daniel approached the changes in his life with a positive attitude—well into his eighties. If anyone had reason to jockey for position, it was Daniel. After all, he had served in the king's court since he was a teenager. He deserved that promotion, but he never sought it. And he certainly did nothing to contrive or manipulate it. He displayed integrity on the job.

Integrity on the Job

Integrity means being honest and trustworthy, even when nobody is looking. Does that describe you when you are working in your job? Daniel 6:4 says that Daniel "was trustworthy and neither corrupt nor negligent." That means that he was known on the job as being a "straight arrow." He could be trusted. He wasn't going to cook the books or steal from his employer. He was a diligent, hard worker.

As often happens in modern work scenarios, these conspirators decided that Daniel had to be removed, so they put a tail on him. They screened his telephone calls and e-mail. They monitored the sites he visited on the Internet. They tried to dig up any garbage from the past they could find. Why, you would have thought that Daniel was running for public office in America! But they couldn't find anything wrong with him. Their only observation was that "he loves God too much."

By the way, when you live for God, there will often be those who are out to get you. They target you because your faithfulness and honesty only accentuate their lack of integrity. Like Daniel, if you decide to be an honest, faithful, diligent employee despite the challenges, God will honor and bless you.

A number of years ago, an elderly man and his wife arrived by train in Chicago. It was a stormy night, and their train had been delayed. It was after midnight when they finally arrived at a downtown hotel they hoped had a vacancy. The young clerk on duty that night, George Boldt, explained that because there were three different conventions in town, their hotel was full, but he would be glad to call around and check with some other hotels. Several calls made clear that no empty rooms were to be found. The young clerk said to the couple, "I can't send a nice couple like you out into the rain on a night like this. Would you be willing to sleep in my room in the basement? It's not large, but it's clean, and I don't need it tonight because I'm on duty."

The couple gladly accepted his offer. The next morning, the man tried to pay George personally, but the young clerk refused. Then the man said to George Boldt, "You're the kind of man who ought to be the boss of the best hotel in America. Maybe one day I'll build one for you." The young clerk only smiled and said, "I was just glad to be of service."

Several years later, George Boldt received a letter with a train ticket to New York City—a gift from the man with whom he had shared his room earlier. When George arrived, the old gentleman took him to the corner of Fifth Avenue and Fifty-fourth Street in Manhattan and said, "This is the hotel I have built for you to manage." George Boldt stared in awe and said, "Are you joking?"

It was no joke. The old man's name was William Waldorf Astor. And that's how George Boldt became the first manager of the Waldorf Astoria Hotel. George's portrait hangs in the lobby today, a tribute to a clerk who showed integrity and went the second mile. What do people say about you when they see you in your job?

Daniel is a great example to us of someone who loved God but was also successful in the workplace. You may be wondering, "Can I be faithful to God and still advance in my career?" Daniel was one of the most successful prime ministers in the history of the world. His job was not just something that he did to put food on the table. He saw his job as a platform upon which he could demonstrate his faith in God. Are you doing that? When people look at you on the job, can they say, "There is a good, faithful, honest, hardworking person who happens to love Jesus"?

The conspirators finally decided to go for the jugular and re-move Daniel by conspiring against his religion. They employed a common strategy in office politics—buttering up the boss. They applied a double coat of flattery to King Darius's pride to con-vince him to send a memo naming himself a virtual "god of the month." No one could pray or worship any other god but Darius for the next thirty days. The idea inflated Darius's ego, so he signed the official decree. When the official memo hit everyone's boxes the next day, the evil scheme was set into motion.

DANIEL'S REACTION TO THE DECREE

Now when Daniel learned that the decree had been published, he went home to his upstairs room where the windows opened toward Jerusalem. Three times a day he got down on his knees and prayed, giving thanks to his God, just as he had done be-fore. Then these men went as a group and found Daniel pray-ing and asking God for help. (Dan. 6:10–11)

Like a bunch of jealous schoolgirls, these leaders ran to the king to tattle on Daniel. Darius found himself backed into a corner. According to their tradition, a law of the Medes and the Persians was unbreakable, and yet Darius was fond of Daniel. To Darius, it was a precarious scenario; to the conspirators, it was a hilarious scene. Their conspiracy had worked just as they had planned.

Notice that Daniel's public life was one of purity and his private life was characterized by prayer. When Daniel learned that it was suddenly against the law to pray, he faced a dilemma. If he had been like many of us, he might have reasoned, "I don't want to cause any political trouble. I will just pray in my heart—after all, you don't have to get on your knees, and you really don't have to pray out loud." No, he decided that he would just keep on praying in his normal fashion. He decided that it was more important to please the God of heaven than to obey the law of man.

This is the second time in this book that we see Daniel handle pressure with prayer. And it is the second time in this book that a child of God commits civil disobedience. Remember, in chapter 3, the king commanded everyone to bow down before the idol. The three Hebrew men conscientiously refused to obey. That's an example of a human government telling you to do something that God's Word forbids, in this case, idolatry. However, this example in chapter 6 is just the opposite. We see a human government forbidding what God has commanded—to pray. Daniel carefully considered the consequences of his civil disobedience, then he broke the law; he prayed anyway. He didn't put on a public display or protest. He didn't pass around a petition to be signed; he just prayed.

If the trend continues in the twenty-first century, our government is going to infringe more and more on our God-given right to pray by telling us where and when we may or may not pray. My advice to you is *pray anyway*—but be prepared to face the consequences. Don't ever be afraid to pray publicly, but ensure that you aren't praying just for show. Public prayer must arise from a faithful, consistent, private prayer life. Don't try to make up for your lack of private prayer by the occasional opportunity for public prayer!

Daniel went to his room and opened the windows toward Jerusalem. He wasn't ashamed to be seen or heard praying. What happened was a spiritual sting operation; he had been "set up." His adversaries were waiting, and they caught him praying. Daniel's prayer, even though it was against the law, made a powerful statement about his devotion to God. Has anyone ever caught you praying? You don't have to "show off" your prayer life—just pray. But you should never be ashamed to pray, and often your prayer will make a powerful impression.

One of my favorite Norman Rockwell prints appeared on the cover of *The Saturday Evening Post* in November 1951. The scene is a greasy, crowded New York restaurant. A grandmother and her young grandson, who are traveling, have been seated at a table inside a dingy roadside café next to a couple of disheveled and road-hardened men. Norman Rockwell has captured the precise moment when the grandmother and her young charge are bowing their heads to pray and give thanks for the food. You can see the men staring in wonder at this sight; someone is praying! It's as if, for that moment, tranquility has descended as the presence of God invaded that noisy café.

How important is prayer to you? Suppose that our government suddenly issued a law saying that you couldn't pray for thirty days. What would you do? If you need some coaching tips regarding the discipline of prayer, consider the following keys to a more dynamic prayer life.

PROVEN PRAYER STRATEGIES

A Specific Place

Daniel had a place where he prayed, his room (6:10). He opened the windows toward Jerusalem. During his time, Jerusalem was only a pile of rubble. But he wasn't praying to Jerusalem; he was praying in faith to the God whom he believed could rebuild Jerusalem.

It helps to have a designated place to have your quiet time. For me, it's a chair in my study. That's where I meet God every morning for prayer and devotional Bible study, not sermon preparation. The Bible indicates that Jesus sought a special place to pray: "Very early in the morning, while it was still dark, Jesus got up, left the house and went off to a solitary place, where he prayed" (Mark

1:35). You need to find a special place where you can get alone with God and meet Him every day.

A Regular Time

Did you notice that Daniel had a regular schedule of praying (6:10)? He did it three times a day, probably based on Psalm 55:17: "Evening, morning, and noon I cry out in distress, and he hears my voice." The Jewish day began with sunset; that is why he started praying in the evening.

For most of us, our day begins in the morning. That's a good time to start. Have a regular time set aside to meet the Lord in prayer. If you don't think you have time to do it in the morning, try setting your clock fifteen minutes earlier. Get up, wake up, and find a place to be alone. Read a psalm, and then start talking to God. Set that time as your regular prayer time. You'll be amazed at the difference it will make in your life.

A Devoted Posture

Notice that Daniel got down on his knees—and he was in his eighties (6:10)! The Bible doesn't command us to kneel when we pray. Several prayer postures are mentioned in the Bible: kneeling, eyes uplifted to heaven, standing, arms raised, or a combination of all of them.

It's interesting that the one posture most of us adopt (bowing our head and closing our eyes) is *never* mentioned in Scripture! The picture of hands pressed together is probably a form of lifting hands to God. I think that kneeling is a good posture because we kneel only to someone to whom we surrender and submit. Some people are too proud to bow their knee to anyone.

In the Garden of Gethsemane the night before He was crucified,

Jesus knelt to pray. Paul also wrote in Ephesians 3:14, "For this reason I kneel before the Father. . . ."

A Consistent Habit

The most important thing that this chapter teaches about Daniel's prayer life is found in the last six words of verse 10. When Daniel got the distressing news about King Darius's decree, he prayed "just as he had done before." That means that, for Daniel, prayer was a regular, consistent habit. It wasn't some kind of emergency mode to which he resorted when trouble arose. He prayed regularly every day—so he was prepared when the emergency came along.

Get into the habit of praying every day. I promise you that Satan will do everything within his power to keep you from praying. Samuel Chadwick once said, "The one concern of the Devil is to keep Christians from praying. He fears nothing from prayerless studies, prayerless work, and prayerless religion. He laughs at our toil, mocks at our wisdom, but he trembles when we pray."

THE LIONS IN DANIEL'S DEN

Then they said to the king, "Daniel, who is one of the exiles from Judah, pays no attention to you, O king, or to the decree you put in writing. He still prays three times a day. . . ." So the king gave the order, and they brought Daniel and threw him into the lions' den. The king said to Daniel, "May your God, whom you serve continually, rescue you!" A stone was brought and placed over the mouth of the den, and the king sealed it with his own signet ring and with the rings of his nobles, so that Daniel's situation might not be changed. (Dan. 6:13, 16–17)

The Persians maintained a torture pit where they kept savage lions to execute prisoners. They took this eighty-year-old saint, tossed him into the pit, and sealed the opening. The conspirators laughed with wicked glee. All they expected to find the next morning was a greasy spot that had once been Daniel, but God had other plans. I've always been fascinated by those lions in Daniel's den because Daniel was really the host, not the guest!

Now, hopefully none of us will ever be tossed before literal lions, but we face a multitude of dangerous situations that appear sometimes as hungry lions. The pressures of life, unpleasant circumstances, and painful situations threaten to consume us. The Bible says that all of us have a foe that is like a lion. First Peter 5:8 says, "Be self-controlled and alert. Your enemy the devil prowls around like a roaring lion looking for someone to devour."

Satan attacks us in many disguises; he even uses other people to attack us. Paul's last letter to Timothy was written not long before he was beheaded by the Romans. He wrote of a time when he was in Ephesus and an evil man named Alexander tried to discredit him. As Paul looked back on this terrible experience, he wrote, "But the Lord stood at my side and gave me strength. . . . And I was delivered from the lion's mouth. The Lord will rescue me from every evil attack and will bring me safely to his heavenly kingdom" (2 Tim. 4:17–18). And the Lord can deliver *you* from the lion's mouth.

While watching the *Animal Planet* channel, I learned that the loudest, most terrifying sound in the jungle is a lion's roar. It will often paralyze a surprised prey. Even so, the main weapon the Devil has is his roar—he wants to scare us with his ferocity. Jesus has rendered Satan toothless and clawless through the Cross, so all he has is a roar. Yet many people are still frightened into spiritual paralysis by his roar.

A friend recently told me the funny joke about a small

congregation that was meeting one Sunday morning. Right in the middle of the service, the Devil burst into the building and started roaring to scare the people. Folks were running out every door and jumping out every window. Even the preacher ran off. The room was empty except for the Devil and one old man, who was sitting there calmly with his arms crossed. The Devil got right in his face and roared again. The man didn't move. The Devil said, "Do you know who I am? Why aren't you afraid of me?" The man looked at him and said, "Yeah, you're the Devil, but I'm not scared of you 'cause I've been married to your sister for forty-five years." You don't have to be afraid of the Devil either. Just be aware that he's out there roaring!

Besides Satan, there are other lions we may face. The lion pit you are in right now might be filled with *relational* lions. Maybe you are going through an ugly divorce or a tough marriage, or you are having trouble with a friend or a family member. You're afraid that this situation will consume you.

Your pit might be filled with *financial* lions. You might be in trouble financially, and you don't know how you're going to make it. Your financial lions are creeping up on you, threatening to devour you.

Or it might be that you are backed up against a wall facing *physical* lions. You've received a bad diagnosis or, worse, you have a nagging health problem and the doctors don't know what it is. You might be struggling with an illness that threatens to end your physical life.

THE LION OF JUDAH

A male lion is known as the king of beasts and typically is more than ten feet long, including his tail, and weighs more than five hundred pounds. A grown male can kill a one hundred-fifty-pound gazelle with one swipe of his paw and can jump over a three-foot fence dangling the gazelle from his mouth. Of all of God's creatures, the lion is one of the most beautiful, fearsome, and majestic creatures. That's why the Bible uses this metaphor to describe the Head Lion, the Lord Jesus.

Revelation 5:5 says, "Then one of the elders said to me, 'Do not weep! See, the *Lion of the Tribe of Judah,* the Root of David, has triumphed'" (emphasis added). In light of this Scripture, let me tell you what I think happened when Daniel was tossed into the pit of lions. He later told Darius that God sent "his angel" to close the mouths of the lions. What do you picture? It could have been some Siegfried and Roy-type angel who tamed them and wrapped a muzzle around each lion's mouth. But perhaps this is the "angel of the Lord," the very same "angel" that walked with Shadrach, Meshach, and Abednego in the fiery furnace. It might have been the preincarnate Christ who visited the lion's pit as the Lion of the Tribe of Judah.

Lions are group oriented. They live and hunt in prides. In each pride is always a dominant male. He's in charge. When he sleeps, the rest of the pride sleeps. When he hunts, the others hunt. When he eats, they all eat. This dominant male, often called the alpha male, is in charge until a new male comes along to challenge him and drive him off.

I believe that on that evening when Daniel was thrown into the lion's den, there was a new boss of the pride: the Lion of the tribe of Judah. In my sanctified imagination, I can picture the new Dominant Lion as He says, "Here kitty, kitty; settle down, fellas. You don't want to eat old Daniel. He is one-half grit and one-half backbone! Besides, you are going to have an all-you-can-eat breakfast buffet tomorrow morning. Oh, and it's a little chilly down here; so, big fella, lie down there so Daniel will have something warm to cuddle up to. One of you let him share your mane so he'll have a soft pillow. And why don't a couple of you swish your tails over his face to keep those flies away?" The Dominant Lion was in charge, and Daniel slept peacefully.

Who had more peace that night, Daniel in the pit of lions or Darius in the palace? Darius had his own lions to fight: the lion of conscience, the lion of guilt, and the lion of accusation. "Then the king returned to his palace and spent the night without eating and without any entertainment being brought to him. And he could not sleep" (Dan. 6:18). He didn't sleep a wink, yet Daniel slept like a baby. What was the difference? Daniel was in the presence of the real King—not the king of beasts, but the King of Kings. He is also called the Prince of Peace. Daniel experienced great peace in the midst of incredible pressure, whereas Darius stayed up all night fighting his own personal lions.

Which scene best describes your life right now? Yes, there are going to be lions on the job, at home, in relationships, with your finances, and in all kinds of trials. Sure, you will be thrown into the pit more than once, but when it happens, be sure that you are in touch with the Dominant Lion, the One who can give you peace in the midst of pressure. Jesus said in John 16:33, "I have told you these things, so that in me you may have peace. In this world you will have trouble. But take heart! I have overcome [dominated] the world."

Jesus Is Still Taming Lions Today

At the first light of dawn, the king got up and hurried to the lions' den. When he came near the den, he called to Daniel in an anguished voice, "Daniel, servant of the living God, has your God, whom you serve continually, been able to rescue you from the lions?" Daniel answered, "O king, live forever! My God sent his angel, and he shut the mouths of the lions. They have not hurt me, because I was found innocent in his sight. Nor have I ever done any wrong before you, O king." The king was overjoyed and gave orders to lift Daniel out of the den. And when Daniel was lifted from the den, no wound was found on him, because he had trusted in his God. At the king's command, the men who had falsely accused Daniel were brought in and thrown into the lions' den, along with their wives and children. And before they reached the floor of the den, the lions overpowered them and crushed all their bones. (Dan. 6:19–24)

To me, the saddest part of the story was when Darius threw the evil men and their families into the lion's pit. The savage lions pounced on them and broke their bones before they could hit the ground. What was the difference between Daniel and these people? They all went into the pit with the same lions. Why did one find peace in the lions' pit while the others were destroyed?

Here's the difference: Daniel had a living, personal relationship with the God of heaven. Daniel carried on a conversation with the God of the universe three times a day, and when he found himself in the pit, God met him even there! These men and their families didn't know God. And there was no peace for them, only agony. If you don't know Jesus Christ, there will be no one to deliver you through the painful experiences of life.

The strength of Daniel's personal success rested on his relationship with God. Daniel is a great example for us—a man who dared to allow God to develop his character in spite of his problems. He wasn't a plastic figure with superficial spirituality. He experienced the ups and downs of life, and we can learn from his life lessons. Daring to be a Daniel in today's world means that we will have the unique experience of seeing God actually forge solid character from the utter chaos in our lives.

Chapter Six

Facing the Future Without Fear

> I make known the end from the beginning,
>> from ancient times, what is still to come.
> I say: My purpose will stand,
>> and I will do all that I please.
>> —Isaiah 46:10

In 1968, a new comedy television show made its debut. It was *Rowan and Martin's Laugh-In*. In 1993, they presented a twenty-five-year anniversary program of the show, showing clips from some of the early episodes. One of the regular features was called "News from the Future," in which two futuristic news anchormen acted as though they were reporting news from decades in the future. It was meant as a spoof, and they tried to be as funny and as outlandish as possible. They forecasted in 1968 that actor Ronald Reagan had been elected president of the United States, and they had another segment in which they reported that the Berlin Wall had fallen. In their attempt at humor, they "predicted" two things that actually came true!

DARING TO BE A DANIEL

Daniel is two books in one. The first part of Daniel (chaps. 1–6) is devoted to personal stories of how Daniel's daring faith affected individuals. However, the second half (chaps. 7–12) is prophetic, including both prophecies that have already been fulfilled and those yet to happen. These prophecies came to Daniel in the form of elaborate visions.

What does Daniel's prophecy teach us about daring to be a Daniel in today's world? Simply this: As we approach the end of time, chaos will increase. If you don't believe that we're close to that time, just compare the modern events we see in the newspaper with the biblical truth revealed in Daniel. In a world filled with violence, wars, and growing despair, we desperately need the character and confidence we find when we focus a watchful and hopeful eye on the future just as he did.

As you examine Daniel 7–12, you must remember that Daniel received these visions around 550 B.C. His prophecies included predictions about the rise of the Greek Empire and the ongoing battles between Egypt and Syria. Much of his prophecy has already come true. For example, chapter 11 in Daniel provides 135 prophetic details, and history confirms that every one of them has been fulfilled precisely. What was prophecy to Daniel's generation is history for us. If anyone ever challenges you about the veracity of the Bible, challenge him or her to study honestly the prophecies of Daniel. Then have them compare the prophecies with how they have been fulfilled in history.

Standing on the other side of many of Daniel's prophecies that have already come true gives us hope that the remaining prophecies in this book will also come to pass. The object of prophecy is not to amaze or confuse us; it's to give us greater hope and confidence in our mighty God, who inspired prophecy. As we look to the future, we recognize there are frightening challenges ahead, but we don't have to be afraid because we know their ultimate outcome.

This section of Daniel is also called apocalyptic literature. If you are unfamiliar with that term, don't feel alone. It is the term from the Greek word *apokalypsis,* which means "unveiling" or "revelation." The last book in the Bible, Revelation, is literally named *Apokalypsis.* Today, apocalyptic literature is used to describe biblical prophecy that "unveils" the future. And for Christians, the greatest future event is the return and reign of Jesus Christ.

A Preview of the Return of Jesus

Christian humorist Dennis Swanburg loves to tell the story of an unforgettable baptism that took place in a little West Texas church. They were building a new sanctuary, and it was almost finished. The new baptistery was functional, although changing rooms were not yet available. Since the changing rooms didn't yet have walls, they hung sheets up so that those who were being baptized could change clothes.

The whole congregation gathered at the start of the service to watch the baptism in the new baptistery. Everything went well until the last person to be baptized made her way down into the water. This lady was terrified of water, even though she had been assured that she had no reason to be concerned. But she panicked in those final seconds before being lowered into the water, clawing the air for anything to keep from going down. Within her grasp was the curtain hung behind the baptistery, which happened to also form the front barrier of the men's changing room. As she reached out in desperation, she pulled down the sheet!

Having just stepped from the baptistery, a man stood with his back to the congregation, wearing nothing but his underwear.

Realizing that something dreadful was wrong, he turned around, only to see the entire congregation gaping at him in astonishment. Assessing the situation quickly, he did the only sensible thing. He dove into the baptistery with the preacher and the panic-stricken woman! Dennis likes to say, "They just dismissed the service after that!"

That's what prophetic Scripture does; it pulls aside the curtain so we can see things that we've never seen before as it relates to Jesus. Daniel unveils a beautiful picture of the Messiah, Jesus Christ.

> In my vision at night I looked, and there before me was one like a son of man, coming with the clouds of heaven. He approached the Ancient of Days [that's God the Father] and was led into his presence. He was given authority, glory and sovereign power; all peoples, nations and men of every language worshiped him. His dominion is an everlasting dominion that will not pass away, and his kingdom is one that will never be destroyed. (Dan. 7:13–14)

> But the court will sit, and his power [that's the little horn—the Antichrist] will be taken away and completely destroyed forever. Then the sovereignty, power and greatness of the kingdoms under the whole heaven will be handed over to the saints [that's when we will reign with Christ on the earth for one thousand years, according to Revelation 20:1–5], the people of the Most High. His kingdom will be an everlasting kingdom, and all rulers will worship and obey him. (Dan. 7:26–27)

The late pastor and extraordinary Bible teacher Ray Stedman comments as follows on this passage in Daniel: "When history reaches its lowest ebb, when the sin of man breaks forth in its most vulgar and most evil forms, then God intends to intervene once again. Jesus will return to set up His kingdom on earth. This is not a mere vagary of Scripture; it is the central teaching of the Word of God. We have as authority to teach this, not only the prophets who spoke of old, but also the apostles of the New Testaments and, even more importantly, the direct testimony of Jesus Christ himself."[1]

The Pinnacle of All Prophecy

By the time of the final vision in Daniel, Daniel was a very old man, well into his eighties. He had retired from government work several years earlier. But even at his advanced age, he was still alive and sensitive spiritually. The same inner zeal burned in his heart that he had experienced as a teenager, even though now he was an old man. This final vision and prophecy that Daniel received covers the final three chapters of this book. It is the longest and most complete prophecy in the entire book.

> At that time I, Daniel, mourned for three weeks. I ate no choice food; no meat or wine touched my lips; and I used no lotions at all until the three weeks were over. On the twenty-fourth day of the first month, as I was standing on the bank of the great river, the Tigris, I looked up and there before me was a man dressed in linen, with a belt of the finest gold around his waist. His body was like chrysolite, his face like lightning, his eyes like flaming torches, his arms and legs like the gleam of burnished bronze, and his voice like the sound of a multitude. I, Daniel, was the only one who saw the vision; the men with me did not see it, but such terror overwhelmed them that they fled and hid themselves. So I was left alone, gazing at this great vision; I had no strength left, my face turned deathly pale and I was helpless.

> Then I heard him speaking, and as I listened to him, I fell into
> a deep sleep, my face to the ground. (Dan. 10:2–9)

Daniel was standing on the bank of the Tigris River with a group of men. When he looked up, he witnessed the most breathtaking sight he had ever seen. He saw a vision of a shining man. Most biblical scholars suggest that this is one of the preincarnate visions of the Lord Jesus Christ.

Daniel alone saw this vision; the men with him were not granted the sight. The others were overwhelmed with the awe of the place and "fled and hid themselves." The main reason many scholars agree that this man was Christ is because the vision that the prophet Daniel received is strikingly identical to the one that the apostle John received on the isle of Patmos. John, too, was an old man when he wrote Revelation.

Compare Daniel's vision to that of John:

> And among the lampstands was someone "like a son of man,"
> dressed in a robe reaching down to his feet and with a golden
> sash around his chest. His head and hair were white like wool,
> as white as snow, and his eyes were like blazing fire. His feet
> were like bronze glowing in a furnace, and his voice was like
> the sound of rushing waters. (Rev. 1:13–15)

In addition, when the apostle Paul was on the road to Damascus, he was arrested by a glimmering vision of Jesus. His traveling companions never saw Christ; only Paul saw Him (Acts 9:3–9). Paul, John, and Daniel all had the same reaction to this vision of the majestic Christ. Paul fell to the ground, blinded by the intensity of the light surrounding Jesus. The apostle John writes, "When I saw Him, I fell at His feet like a dead man" (Rev. 1:17 NASB). In verses 8–9, Daniel describes how he became weak and collapsed to the ground, landing face downward. Let me assure you when you see Jesus face to face that will be your reaction as well. You will fall to the ground in the presence of His awesome glory. Of all of the visions of Jesus that are contained in the book of Daniel, this vision is the most majestic.

The Primary Point of Prophecy

The primary point of prophecy is to present a clearer picture of the Lord Jesus Christ. People who are "prophecy junkies" often read the Bible to try to find the details of the future so they can create a new chart or some new end-time prediction. They miss the whole point. The more one studies prophecy, the more one sees that the pinnacle of all prophecy is Jesus. Don't forget that the last book in our Bible is not called "Revelations" as most people call it. It is "The Revelation." However, the full title, according to Revelation 1:1, is "The Revelation of Jesus Christ." Jesus is the point of all prophecy. The more you study prophecy, the more clearly you will see Jesus.

This was not the first time Daniel had been exposed to Jesus. In Daniel 2:34, Jesus was the stone not cut by human hands that crushed the kingdoms of this world. In Daniel 7:13, Jesus was called the "son of man" who is given an everlasting kingdom. In Daniel 8:25, He is called the "Prince of princes" who comes to defeat the Antichrist. In Daniel 9:26, Jesus is identified as the "Anointed One" (Messiah) who will be cut off 483 years after the decree goes forth to rebuild Jerusalem. And in chapter 3, Jesus is the fourth man who walked in the fire with Daniel's three Hebrew friends.

Have you learned the most important tool for interpreting the Bible? Here it is: the entire Bible is all about Jesus. You can find Jesus from Genesis 1:1 all the way to Revelation 22:21 and on every page in between. If you read the Bible (especially the Old

Testament) and don't find Jesus, you'd better read it again because you've missed the point.

Turn Your Eyes upon Jesus

> I looked up and there before me was a man dressed in linen, with a belt of the finest gold around his waist. His body was like chrysolite, his face like lightning, his eyes like flaming torches, his arms and legs like the gleam of burnished bronze, and his voice like the sound of a multitude. (Dan. 10:5–6)

His Clothing Speaks of Royalty

His white linen robe is a symbol of the purity and holiness of Jesus. In ancient times, only a king would wear a golden sash. So we see Jesus pictured as the King of Kings and Lord of Lords.

His Body Is Beautiful Beyond Description

The NIV describes His body as "chrysolite." The King James uses the word *beryl*. The Hebrew word describes a very rare, precious stone that came from only one place on earth—modern Spain. It was more valuable than diamonds; it was a transparent, shimmering stone. This just means that the overall appearance of the body of Jesus was too beautiful to describe. Even so, the body of Christ, the church, is beautiful beyond description.

His Face Reveals His Radiance

Brilliant light is associated with the countenance of Jesus. First John 1:5 says, "God is light, and in him is no darkness at all" (KJV). In Exodus 34:29–30, when Moses was exposed to the afterglow of

God's glory on Mount Sinai, he came down from the mountain with a face that was shining; he probably looked as though his face was sunburned!

His Eyes Burn Through Any Pretense

The eyes of Jesus are like flaming torches. As we say, His eyes can "burn right through you." In Luke's gospel, we read that on the night that Peter denied Christ, Jesus was being moved from one area to another in the house of Caiaphas. Peter was still standing in the courtyard. As Jesus had predicted, there was the sound of a rooster crowing, and "The Lord turned and looked straight at Peter" (Luke 22:61). Can't you imagine that His look burned into Peter's heart? In one split second, that fiery-hot gaze communicated what Jesus was saying: "Peter, I told you that you would deny me three times, but I still love you." That's why Peter went out and wept bitterly. The Lord Jesus sees what nobody else can see. He can see into the very depths of your heart.

His Arms Are Strong to Comfort

His arms are described as burnished bronze—that speaks of strength. I love the time when Jesus called the little children to Himself (Mark 10:13–16; Luke 18:15–17). The Bible says that He picked them up in His arms and just held them to show them that He loved them. Those were the same arms that fashioned the universe into existence, the same arms that grew strong from working in a carpenter's shop. They are the same strong arms that hold the universe together and the same arms that reach out to you today. They are the same arms that were stretched out on a wooden cross to embrace my sin and your sin. What strength! What tenderness!

His Feet Enable Him to Walk over Danger

Bronze also speaks of durability and protection. It is dangerous to walk in a lot of places, but if your feet are like bronze it is no problem. Bronze symbolizes the beautiful feet of Jesus that walked the dusty roads of Galilee and over the stormy waters of the Sea of Galilee. Ephesians 1:22 says that "God placed *all* things under His feet" (emphasis added). So don't be afraid; if you are walking with Jesus you will always be safe.

His Voice Is Too Loud to Ignore

Daniel describes His voice as being "like the sound of a multitude." Have you ever been to a college or pro football game when thousands of fans are yelling? It is a sound that you'll never forget. Sure, God sometimes speaks to us in a still, small voice, but the voice of the glorified, exalted Christ is louder than a hundred jetliners taking off. His voice is too loud for you to ignore.

IN THE END

Since I was a little boy, I have loved to read. I grew up reading all of the Hardy Boys mystery novels. Frank and Joe Hardy were always getting into terrible situations in which they risked life or limb. I would often be engrossed in one of their exciting adventures when my mother would tell me to turn off my light and go to sleep. But I couldn't leave Joe and Frank hanging on the edge of a cliff with rocks below and a huge, angry bear above! So I would often just flip over to the last page and read that Joe and Frank were sitting down with their parents for a delicious meal. Then I could shut the book and go to sleep because I had read the last chapter, and I knew that they were going to be okay. I didn't know all of the details of *how* they were going to escape danger and death; I just knew they were!

God has given us a glimpse of the last chapter of His plan. Things are bad, and they are going to get worse. Amid the chaos, however, Jesus is going to return and deal with all of the sin and wickedness that has plagued this planet. He will establish His kingdom. He will come and set everything right! We don't know all of the details of how and when it will happen, but we can rest assured that God's plan will be victorious.

Chapter Seven

Confession *Is* Good for the Soul

I prayed to the LORD my God and confessed: "O Lord, the great and awesome God, who keeps his covenant of love with all who love him and obey his commands, we have sinned and done wrong. We have been wicked and have rebelled; we have turned away from your commands and laws."

—Daniel 9:4–5

The backdrop of Daniel's personal life was a time similar to today—a world of major uncertainties. These included pluralism, religious persecution, and theological and religious liberalism. However, things didn't seem to get much better as he took a privileged look at the future—the world in which we live today. He encountered mass fear, war, idolatry, deceit, and political upheaval. However, Daniel turned the potential for personal chaos and the craziness of his culture into opportunities to discover hope. Despite the horrific events in his visions, he glimpsed a certain future. How did he do it? His strategy began with confession.

DANIEL'S REACTION

Daniel's reaction to these prophetic revelations is recorded in Daniel 9:4–5, where he offered a prayer of confession. Confession, by the way, *is* good for your soul. Most of us are much better at excusing our sins and mistakes than confessing them. We are quick to point out other peoples' mistakes, but we have a hard time admitting when we have blown it. Some of our excuses must certainly sound comical to God. Speaking of lame excuses, here are some actual excerpts from reports to insurance companies in which individuals explained why they had an automobile accident:

- The other guy was all over the road, and I had to swerve a number of times before I hit him.
- The pedestrian had no idea which direction to go, so when he hesitated, I ran over him.
- The telephone pole approached my car at a rapid speed, and as I swerved to get out of its way, it hit me.

Like these drivers, we tend to try to excuse our mistakes rather than confess them to God. As we begin this chapter, let me ask you a very personal question. On a scale of 1 to 5, how would you rate your personal prayer life, with (1) meaning "no understanding or practice of prayer" and (5) meaning "flourishing prayer life"? Go ahead. Be honest. How effective and consistent is your prayer life right now?

Dr. S. D. Gordon once wrote,

The greatest thing we can do for God and man is to pray. It is not the only thing, but it is the chief thing. The great people of the earth are the people who pray. I do not mean those who talk about prayer; nor those who say they believe in prayer; nor yet those who can explain about prayer; but I mean those who take time to pray. They have not the time. It must be taken from something else. . . . It is wholly a secret service. I often think that sometimes we pass some plain-looking woman quietly slipping out of church. We hardly give her a passing thought and we do not know or guess that she is the one who is doing more for her church, and for the world and for God than a hundred others who claim more attention, because she prays, truly prays as the Spirit of God inspires and guides.[1]

Pray According to the Bible (9:1–2)

We read in Daniel 9:2, "In the first year of his [Darius's] reign, I, Daniel, understood from the Scriptures, according to the word of the LORD given to Jeremiah the prophet, that the desolation of Jerusalem would last seventy years." Daniel had a copy of some of the writings that we call the Old Testament. He was able to read prophecy and interpret it literally. That is exactly what we are doing here with Daniel's prophecy. We can read the same words that caused Daniel to understand that the captivity of the Jews would end after seventy years.

> "When seventy years are completed for Babylon, I will come to you and fulfill my gracious promise to bring you back to this place. For I know the plans I have for you," declares the LORD, "plans to prosper you and not to harm you, plans to give you hope and a future. Then you will call upon me and come and pray to me, and I will listen to you." (Jer. 29:10–12)

Daniel understood the Scripture spoken through Jeremiah, and he discerned his current time. We know that he had been taken captive around 605 B.C., and this was the first year of Darius's reign (in 538 B.C.). So by this time, Daniel had been in captivity for sixty-seven years. He recognized that his people were only three years away from returning to Jerusalem. He also realized that they were not prepared spiritually, so simply reading and understanding the Word of God drove him to his knees in prayer. As we read God's Word in light of current events, can we say that we are prepared for what is sure to come? Reading God's Word should drive us to our knees in prayer.

Andrew Murray wrote, "Little of the Word with little prayer is death to the spiritual life. Much of the Word with little prayer gives a sickly life. Much prayer with little of the Word gives emotional life. But a full measure of both the Word and prayer each day gives a healthy and powerful life."[2]

A maturing Christian understands the dynamic connection between God's Word, the Bible, and prayer. In His Word, God tells us what He is going to do, and then He tells us to pray that it will happen! Sadly, many people are confused at this point. They say, "Well, if God is going to do it, there is nothing for me to do. So I'll just sit and watch it happen." Then, when nothing happens, they think that God must be unfaithful to His promise. However, God is faithful. The problem is that we have not responded to the part that God gives us to do. Prayer is God's way of involving us in the program He sets out to do. That's why Jesus instructed us to pray, "Your will be done on earth as it is in heaven" (Matt. 6:10). Pray for His will to be done—and then *do* it!

We must get rid of the notion that prayer is a way of making God work for us. Most of us think of prayer that way. We realize that we have needs. We want something done, something that we find to be beyond our ability to handle with our own strength, so we rely on the promises of God. We come before Him and say, "God, You said that You would do whatever I ask. This is what I want You to do." By that approach, we are implying that God is like a heavenly bellhop; when we push the prayer button, He is to show up and take orders for what we want Him to do. But that is to misunderstand totally the nature and purpose of prayer. No, prayer is God's way of involving us in what He intends to do.

You should always pray with an open Bible and an open heart. As you read what God is saying, start doing what He tells you to do. People sometimes ask me, "How can I know that I am praying according to God's will? Do I just ask for whatever and then add on the end, 'If it is your will'?" That's such a faithless way to pray. The way to know with absolute certainty that you are praying according to God's will is to pray according to God's Word. God's plan is often not put into action until His people pray and then carry out His plan.

Pray with Humility in Attitude and Action (9:3)

Daniel 9:3 says, "So I turned to the Lord God and pleaded with him in prayer and petition, in fasting, and in sackcloth and ashes." Daniel took off his beautiful oriental robes and jewelry and donned a simple gown of rough burlap. He then took ashes and covered his head and body. The term *sackcloth* is used forty-six times in the Bible. It is often combined with the word *ashes*. These were symbols of deep grief and mourning. When a family member died, the grieving relative wore sackcloth, a rough, irritating garment of the coarsest material. The constant irritation of wearing that garment spoke of the inner pain that the person felt. Today, people often wear black for mourning to reflect that their lives have been robbed of color by their grief.

In contrast, spreading dirty ashes on one's head was a statement of guilt. When you are covered with soot and ashes, it's impossible to feel clean. Ashes represent something previous that is burned or lost. It is a symbol of deep repentance. Many Christians who follow the liturgical calendar observe Ash Wednesday and have a small smudge of ash rubbed onto their foreheads to prepare themselves for forty days of anticipation and repentance before Easter. (Ash Wednesday is always forty days before Easter, not counting Sundays.) In the Bible, rather than a single smudge, the penitent person covered his or her entire body with filthy ashes. Basically, when you wear sackcloth and are covered with dirty ashes, you aren't comfortable and you don't feel clean. It is an outward expression of your inward pain and agony.

Fasting is another act of humility that enhances prayer. When you refrain from eating food or certain foods for a period of time, it allows you to maintain a prayer goal in your mind. In the Bible, fasting was never practiced simply to lose weight; it was always connected with prayer. As you forego food, it reminds you to pray for your specific prayer burden. Jesus fasted and prayed, and He instructed us to fast and pray as well.

Fasting should always be done privately with no announcement or fanfare. If you think it makes you seem to be "more holy" to mention to someone that you're fasting, you might as well pig out on a donut; you've spoiled the point of your fast. Jesus told us that when we pray and fast, nobody should know about it but our heavenly Father. Fasting also teaches you to say "no" to your bodily appetites, which is a good exercise for all of us.

We must be careful that we never do these acts of humility to impress others. Jesus said, "When you fast, do not look somber as the hypocrites do, for they disfigure their faces to show men they are fasting. I tell you the truth, they have received their reward in full. But when you fast, put oil on your head [wash and fix your hair] and wash your face, so that it will not be obvious to men that you are fasting, but only to your Father, who is unseen; and your Father, who sees what is done in secret, will reward you" (Matt. 6:16–18).

I heard a funny story of some children who were asked to bring a symbol of their faith to kindergarten for show and tell. The little Jewish boy brought a Star of David, and a little Catholic girl brought a rosary. Next, a little Baptist boy brought a casserole. It's a cute story, but the point is sad; most Christians do much more "feasting" than fasting. However, fasting is not just a Catholic thing or an Old Testament concept. According to Jesus, it is an act of humility that God notices and rewards.

Our humility should be on display for God only, not for human observation. When we are humble before God, others might observe our humility, but we aren't doing it for their sakes; it's for God. Have you ever put on sackcloth and ashes? Have you ever fasted? If you have, don't tell me or you've spoiled it. But if you wonder why your prayers don't seem to be getting past the light bulbs, perhaps you should try these acts of humility.

The well-known preacher Charles Spurgeon once said, "Proud prayers may knock their heads on mercy's lintel, but they can never pass through the portal. You cannot expect anything of God unless you put yourself in the right place, that is, as a beggar at his footstool; then will He hear you, and not until then."[3]

Pray with Intensity but Brevity (9:3–4)

In verse 3, Daniel said that he "pleaded with [the Lord]." The Hebrew word translated *pleaded* suggests "to wrestle," as Jacob did with the angel in Genesis 32. Then Daniel said, "I prayed to the Lord my God and confessed" (Dan. 9:4). In Hebrew, the word *prayed* is an emphatic imperative denoting extreme intensity. Daniel wasn't merely offering a casual prayer; he was praying fervently.

Ten times Daniel addressed God as "O Lord" or "O my God." The word *O* is an untranslatable word that represents a groan. Romans 8:26 says that when we are praying "in the Spirit" we may be so burdened that we may express groans that can't be uttered. Have you ever agonized in prayer? Have you wrestled and groaned in prayer?

James 5:16 says that "the effective, fervent prayer of a righteous man avails much" (NKJV). We can learn from Daniel that for a prayer to be intense, it doesn't have to be lengthy. We can read Daniel's entire prayer in about two and a half minutes. Throughout the Bible, we see that prayers don't have to be interminable to be effective. The longest recorded prayer of Jesus is found in John 17 and can be read aloud in three minutes. The model prayer (sometimes called the Lord's Prayer) that Jesus taught us to pray can be spoken in less than thirty seconds.

Nineteenth-century American evangelist D. L. Moody didn't care for long public prayers. At his citywide crusades, a local pastor was always asked to give a public prayer. If the prayer started going too long, Moody would interrupt the pastor and say to the congregation, "While our Brother catches up on his prayer life, we are going to continue with the service!" Word soon got around, and there were few long prayers after that!

Confess Personal and National Sins Specifically (9:4–13)

Let's join Daniel in his prayer closet and eavesdrop on his prayer. Picture a dignified man in his mid-eighties, wearing coarse sackcloth. His head and body have been polluted with filthy ashes; he's been fasting. He's down on his knees, as was his custom according to Daniel 6:10. I can almost hear him weeping as he begins pouring out his heart to God in 9:4:

> O Lord, the great and awesome God, who keeps his covenant
> of love with all who love him and obey his commands [prayer
> should always start with praise stating God's glorious charac-

ter], we have sinned and done wrong. We have been wicked and have rebelled; we have turned away from your commands and laws. We have not listened to your servants the prophets, who spoke in your name to our kings, our princes and our fathers, and to all the people of the land. (Dan. 9:4–6)

He didn't make excuses; instead, he admitted that the nation of Israel had gotten just what it deserved. He continued in verse 13, "Just as it is written in the Law of Moses, all this disaster has come upon us, yet we have not sought the favor of the Lord our God by turning from our sins and giving attention to your truth." This is the kind of prayer that needs to be prayed in America today!

Then his prayer concluded in verse 18 with a crescendo of intensity as he implored God to act. "Give ear, O God, and hear; open your eyes and see the desolation of the city that bears your Name. We do not make requests of you because we are righteous, but because of your great mercy. O Lord, listen! O Lord, forgive! O, Lord, hear and act! For your sake, O my God, do not delay, because your city and your people bear your Name."

Wow! This has to be the MVP (Most Valuable Prayer) of the Old Testament. If you are committed to being a Daniel, you'll need to learn how to confess your sins.

Personal Sins

When you read Daniel's prayer, you notice that his confession was both personal and collective. He both spoke about his sin and took responsibility for his people. He didn't say, "Oh, Lord *they* have sinned." He said, "*We* have sinned." Have you ever noticed how easy it is to confess other people's sin? Daniel recognized that he was part of a group that God was punishing for their collective sins. When one football lineman jumps offside, the entire team is

penalized. Although Daniel might not have been personally re-
sponsible for the sins that caused his people to be penalized by
being sent into Babylon for seventy years, he took responsibility.
Have you taken personal responsibility for not only your sins but
also the immorality of our culture?

We are much better at making excuses than confessing sin. We
live in a "no-fault" culture in which we are offered "no-fault" insurance and "no-fault" divorce. The mantra of our culture is, "Hey,
it's not my fault." We have come up with pretty names to excuse
our sin. What we call an "affair" God calls "adultery." What we call
"a little weakness" God calls "wickedness." What we call "a mis-
take" God calls "madness." Proverbs 28:13 says, "He who conceals
his sins does not prosper, but whoever confesses and renounces
them finds mercy."

Do you spend time regularly confessing your personal sins to
Jesus, or do you spend more time concealing your sins from others? You say, "I can't think of any sins right now." Just start guess-
ing; you'll usually be right on target every time. If you still can't
think of any, start by confessing the sin of prayerlessness for our
nation. Samuel said, "God forbid that I should sin against the Lord
in ceasing to pray for you" (1 Sam. 12:23 KJV). Have you confessed
and repented of the sin of not praying for your church and your
nation as you should?

Daniel did more than confess his sins; he was willing to repent.
The Old Testament word for repent means "a change of mind that
produces a change in behavior." No true confession is possible
without repentance. They are spiritual conjoined twins that can't
be separated. If you assume that you can continue to sin and then
simply run to God and say, "Oops! I did it again. Please forgive
me," then you don't understand the holiness of God. Confession
without repentance is just uttering shallow words with no
meaning.

National Sins

True confession always starts with the general and then proceeds to the specific. Notice that Daniel said in verse 5, "we have sinned and done wrong." That's general. Then he gives some specific examples of how they had sinned:

- "We have . . . rebelled" (v. 5).
- "We have turned away from your commands and laws" (v. 5).
- "We have not listened to your servants the prophets" (v. 6).
- "All Israel has transgressed your law [we have stepped over your line] and turned away, refusing to obey you" (v. 11).

Daniel admitted that the reason they were in such a mess was their own fault. He didn't shake his fist in God's face and say, "Why, Lord are you being so mean to me?" True confession is always *honest* and *specific.* Where did we get the idea that we could simply offer a general prayer of "blanket confession"? We want to pray, "Oh Lord, forgive all of my sins and forgive the sins of my nation while you're at it. Okay, amen, that's done." It's important to be *specific* with God because confession isn't informing God of your specific sins; it is *agreeing* with God that the things you have thought, done, and said are wrong. No excuses.

In the model prayer, Jesus taught us to pray, "Forgive us our debts [sins]." However, He wasn't teaching us a formula for confession. His next statement was, *"as* we also have forgiven our debtors" (Matt. 6:12). He was teaching us that we do not have the luxury of holding unforgiveness in our hearts if we ever need the forgiveness of God. Start agreeing with God that some of your actions and the tragic sins of our nation are hideous before His holy character.

The national sins of America are public sins that we need to confess publicly. Daniel's prayer became a public prayer—we are reading it today—because it involved the national sin of Israel's rebellion. When Daniel recognized that the Jews were guilty of sinning against a holy God, he fell to his face to beg for God's mercy and forgiveness. That's what we need to do for our nation.

Chuck Colson, advisor to President Nixon at the height of Watergate and founder of Prison Fellowship Ministries, wrote,

> I spent the first half of my professional life in politics and public service. . . . I really believed that people could be changed by government being changed. But I never looked beyond government into the hearts of people. . . . But when I became a Christian, I gained a new perspective on the actual influence political structures have on the course of history. I began to see that societies are changed only when people are changed, not the other way around. America's crisis is not political, it's moral and spiritual.[4]

As Daniel cried out to God for mercy, he referred to Jerusalem as a reproach to all of the nations. America has become an international "reproach" in our time. We were once known for decency, goodness, and fairness. Today we are the chief exporters of violence, pornography, rock music, drugs, and sexual immorality.

When minister Joe Wright was asked to open the new session of the Kansas Senate with prayer, everyone was expecting the usual placid generalities. Instead, he prayed a prayer that lasted a little more than sixty seconds, but it was so brutally honest that it enraged many of the Kansas senators.

> Heavenly Father, we come before you today to ask Your forgiveness and to seek Your direction and guidance. Your Word

says, 'Woe to those who call evil good' but that is exactly what we have done. We have lost our spiritual equilibrium and reversed our values. We confess that we have ridiculed the absolute truth of Your Word and called it Pluralism; we have endorsed perversion and called it an alternative lifestyle; we have exploited the poor and called it the lottery; we have rewarded laziness and called it welfare; we have killed our unborn and called it choice; we have shot abortionists and called it justifiable; we have neglected to discipline our children and called it building self-esteem; we have abused power and called it politics; we have coveted our neighbor's possessions and called it ambition; we have polluted the air with profanity and pornography and called it freedom of expression; we have ridiculed the time-honored values of our forefathers and called it enlightenment. Search us, Oh, God, and know our hearts today; cleanse us from every sin and set us free. We ask it in the name of Your Son, the living Savior, Jesus Christ. Amen.

—Minister Joe Wright,
opening session, Kansas Senate,
January 23, 1996

That's a brave, bold prayer. But it's the kind of prayer that all of us need to be praying. When was the last time you confessed to God the national sins of immorality, abortion, and racial discrimination? Healing won't come to our land until we start confessing our personal and national sins to God.

Ask for God's Glory, Not Your Gain (9:15–19)

Daniel told God that his prayer was "for your sake" (9:17). Effective praying is always for God's sake—not ours. Many of our prayers are what I call "Polly-want-a-cracker prayers." We come to God and basically say, "Gimme, gimme, gimme!" Daniel prayed his prayer for the return and rebuilding of his nation. Yet Daniel died before these events were fully implemented. We have no record that he ever returned to the land of his childhood. He wasn't praying for himself; He was praying for God's glory.

James 4:3 says, "When you ask, you do not receive, because you ask with wrong motives, that you may spend what you get on your pleasures." That might be one reason why your prayers seem ineffective. When you pray, don't just bring a grocery list to God saying, "Go down the aisles of heaven and fill my basket with these particular blessings." Instead, ensure that you pray with the glory of God, not your personal gain, as your reward.

Expect an Answer Before You Finish (9:20–23)

When you pray, always expect an answer. One of the best ways to pray in faith is to thank God *before* you see the answer. It doesn't require faith to thank God for His answer once it has already arrived. A friend of mine was once going through a difficult life struggle involving her health and marriage and shared this remarkable prayer with me:

> Dear God:
> I want to thank You for what You have already done. I am not going to wait until I see results or receive rewards, I am thanking You right now.
> I am not going to wait until I feel better or things look better, I am thanking You right now.
> I am not going to wait until people say they are sorry or until they stop talking about me, I am thanking You right now.
> I am not going to wait until the pain in my body disappears, I am thanking You right now.

I am not going to wait until my financial situation improves, I am going to thank You right now.

I am not going to wait until the children are grown and the house is quiet, I am going to thank You right now.

I am not going to wait until I get promoted at work or until I get the job, I am going to thank You right now.

I am not going to wait until I understand every experience in my life that has caused me pain or grief, I am going to thank You right now.

I am not going to wait until the journey gets easier or the challenges are removed. I am thanking You right now.

I am thanking You because I am alive. I am thanking You because I made it through the day's difficulties.

I am thanking You because I have walked around the obstacles.

I am thanking You because I have the ability and the opportunity to do more and do better.

I am thanking You because despite my imperfect ways, You continue to bless me.

I am thanking You because You have not given up on me.

Some prayers are answered instantly, but that's not always the case. We are going to see in Daniel chapter 10 that God's answer to prayer is sometimes delayed. The point is to pray expectantly—believing that God will ultimately hear and respond. However, it's exciting when we pray and God answers us before we get up off our knees. That's what happened with Daniel in this prayer.

Daniel reported in verses 20–21, "While I was speaking and praying, confessing my sin and the sin of my people Israel and making my request to the Lord my God for his holy hill—while I was still in prayer, Gabriel, the man [Gabriel is an angel, and ordinary angels most often appear as men] I had seen in the earlier vision, came to me [the Hebrew word is *na-ga*, which means 'to reach out and touch'] in swift flight about the time of the evening sacrifice."

Daniel hadn't completed his prayer before a soft hand touched him. He looked up, and there stood Gabriel in the form of a man. Daniel must have thought, *That was quick!* Actually, it was much quicker than Daniel realized, for as soon as he began to pray, God commanded Gabriel to respond. The answer to prayer is often faster than the speed of thought! In Isaiah 65:24, God gives an amazing promise: "Before they call I will answer; while they are still speaking I will hear." Like Daniel, start *expecting* God to answer your prayers, and you will find that His grace is revealed to you in multiple ways.

God *always* answers prayer. If your request is wrong, God simply answers, "No." If you aren't right with God when you pray, His answer is, "Grow." If the timing of your request is not right, God says, "Slow." But when the request is right, you are right with God, and the timing is right, God says, "Go—claim it!"

In the next chapter, we'll examine what Gabriel teaches Daniel about spiritual warfare and spiritual victory.

Chapter Eight

Spiritual Battle Stations

Then he [the angel Gabriel] continued, "Do not be afraid, Daniel. Since the first day that you set your mind to gain understanding and to humble yourself before your God, your words were heard, and I have come in response to them."

—Daniel 10:12

WHAT IS SPIRITUAL WARFARE?

Daniel's conversation with the angel Gabriel in Daniel 10 gives us a glimpse of what takes place behind the scenes of this physical world. He enables us to look into the invisible spiritual world of how the good angels of God and the fallen angels of Satan interact.

Several years ago, I wrote a book on angels called *Do Angels Really Exist?*[1] Several thousand copies have been sold around America, and I still am called upon to conduct telephone interviews for radio stations. Why? Because angels are a fascinating topic, and ignorance about them is widespread. Hebrews 1:14 teaches us that angels are God's "ministering spirits sent to serve those who will inherit salvation." But the ministry of angels isn't confined to the pages of Scripture. There are thousands of contemporary "angel stories" in which people believe that God sent an angel to protect them.

During World War II, soldiers were often given small Bibles to take into battle. A veteran once showed me his Bible. A German bullet had punctured it and passed halfway through until it stopped in Psalm 91. The veteran pointed to Psalm 91:11, which says, "For he will command his angels concerning you to guard you in all your ways." The ministry of angels is continually occurring, although we are not aware of what is happening. What we think are ordinary coincidences are often the result of the ministry of angels.

When Daniel encountered the angel on the banks of the Tigris River, he said, "A hand touched me and set me trembling on my hands and knees. He [the angel] said, 'Daniel, you who are highly esteemed, consider carefully the words I am about to speak to you, and stand up, for I have now been sent to you.' And when he said this to me, I stood up trembling" (Dan. 10:10–11).

Gabriel had visited Daniel before to explain an earlier vision, so this was his second message to God's man.

> Then he continued, "Do not be afraid, Daniel. Since the first day that you set your mind to gain understanding and to humble yourself before your God, your words were heard, and I have come in response to them. But the prince of the Persian kingdom resisted me twenty-one days. [He's not talking about a human prince here but a fallen angel, a demon.] Then Michael, one of the chief princes [Michael is the archangel], came to help me, because I was detained there with the king of Persia. Now I have come to explain to you what will happen to your people in the future, for the vision concerns a time yet to come." (Dan. 10:12–14)

So he said, "Do you know why I have come to you? Soon I will return to fight against the prince of Persia, and when I go, the prince of Greece will come; but first I will tell you what is written in the Book of Truth. (No one supports me against them except Michael, your prince.)" (Dan. 10:20–21)

God sent His angel to Daniel to do two things for him. First, he came to comfort and reassure Daniel. In verses 12 and 19, he said, "Do not be afraid." When you isolate all of the messages that angels deliver in the Bible, the one message they deliver more than any other is, "Don't be afraid!"

The second thing Gabriel came to do was to deliver the answer to Daniel's prayer. As we study this process, we learn something about the mystery of prayer that is of critical importance if we are going to be a Daniel in today's world.

POWERFUL PRAYER

Prayer Starts with a Burden (10:2–3)

Daniel was so burdened that he began a semi-fast. He stopped eating meat, drinking wine, and went without using body lotion to soften the effects of living in the dry desert. He might have been living on bread and water. He was disturbed because, according to the timing of this vision, the Jews should have already returned to Jerusalem. But history records that many of the Jews had grown so accustomed to the lifestyle of Persia that they decided to stay. The story of Esther reported that many Jews were living in Persia after they had been given the right to return to their homeland. Daniel was so distressed because he saw that his people had fallen in love with the wrong world—Persia, the land of idolatry and immorality, instead of Israel, God's promised land!

As you read these words, are you burdened for America? Are you alarmed to see our culture embracing degradation and moral filth? Are you so burdened that, like Daniel, you are fasting and praying regularly? Sadly, too many of us aren't disturbed because American Christians are in love with our godless culture. Daniel fasted and prayed for three weeks. Shouldn't we consider doing the same?

Prayer Doesn't Stop Until an Answer Comes (10:12)

Daniel didn't pray just once and then say, "There, I've done my duty. I've talked to God about this problem." No, he humbled himself before God, and he carried a heavy spirit of mourning for three weeks. Gabriel reported to Daniel that his prayer had been heard since the first day he prayed (10:12). However, the answer had not yet come, so Daniel kept praying in faith for three more weeks. "Give me understanding," he had cried. Still, nothing came. So, he kept praying.

For twenty-one days, he petitioned God—wrestling, agonizing, weeping, and waiting—all the time unaware that a battle was raging in the unseen realm of the heavens. Daniel's answer was delayed because Satan's forces fought against his prayer. If Daniel's persistence in prayer had not outlasted this period of delay, he might not have received his answer. The key factor was his perseverance and his determination to keep praying until the answer came. The reason the Bible tells us to persist in prayer is *not* to overcome God's reluctance but to *prevail* against Satan's opposition.

I'm convinced that too many of us stop praying before God sends an answer. We suppose that just because we haven't gotten an instant answer that "it's not God's will," so we stop praying. That's not the Bible way of praying. We are told to pray and to keep praying. When Jesus taught His disciples about prayer, He used a present tense verb that signified a continuous action. For instance, what Jesus said in Matthew 7:7 should be translated as follows: "Ask (and keep on asking), and it will be given to you; seek (and keep on seeking), and you will find; knock (and keep on knocking), and the door will be opened to you." Is there some area in your life in which you have stopped praying because you haven't gotten an instant answer? Why did you stop praying?

Prayer Is Often Resisted by Satan's Soldiers (10:13)

There are reasons why the answer to our prayers may be delayed. Verse 13 gives us tremendous insight into the "battle of prayer" that takes place in the invisible, spiritual world around us. We learn from this passage that Satan, our adversary, fights to keep our prayers from being answered. Satan is sly, subtle, and sinister; he wants to make your life miserable.

Gabriel revealed to Daniel that he had been delayed by the prince of Persia (a demon). However, Michael (the archangel), one of the chief princes, helped him. In verse 20, the angel related that he was going to fight against this prince of Persia. That's warfare language. Don't forget, the Devil has a highly organized, demonized, mobilized army. He assigns demons to certain nations and governments to try to influence them for evil. Just as there was a prince of Persia, I'm convinced that there is a "prince of America" who devotes much of his attention to our political leaders in Washington. It is logical to assume that a "prince of Iraq," a "prince of Afghanistan," and a "prince of Russia" exist as well.

Because of this invisible warfare, the apostle Paul wrote, "Put on the full armor of God so that you can take your stand against the devil's schemes. For our struggle is not against flesh and blood, but against the rulers, against the authorities, against the powers of this dark world and against the spiritual forces of evil in the heavenly realms. .... [And what do you do once you are dressed in this armor?] And *pray* in the Spirit on all occasions with all kinds of prayers and requests" (Eph. 6:11–12, 18a).

In his excellent book *Engaging the Enemy: How to Fight and Defeat Territorial Spirits*, Dr. Peter Wagner shares that as we move into the twenty-first century, the Holy Spirit is calling the church to spiritual warfare with territorial spirits—evil spirits, demons, principalities, powers, and world rulers of this present darkness. Our enemies are the evil "princes" who are assigned to specific territories, regimes, or institutions.

Pastor John Piper writes,

> The New Testament tells us that this prince of demons "darkens the minds of unbelievers" (2 Cor. 4:4), and that he "deceives the world" (Rev. 12:9), and that he plants his weeds (unbelievers) throughout the world (Matt. 13:39), and that he takes people captive to do his will (2 Tim. 2:25), and that he plucks up the seed of the Word when it is preached (Matt. 13:4). Since we know the prince of demons does all that, we may conclude that this is what his sub-princes do as well. So then, I would conclude that there are high-ranking demonic powers over various regimes and dominions and governments and realms of the world; and that they work to create as much evil and corruption and spiritual darkness as they can.[2]

Daniel 10 makes clear that spiritual warfare is a reality. When we read about the incredible atrocities of Hitler, Stalin, the leaders of the Bosnian-Serbian conflict, and, more recently, the Taliban in Afghanistan, we cannot escape the fact that there is a Devil who is bent on the destruction of the human race. Satan has ruined everything he has ever touched. He will try to wreck your life if you don't resist him. Our only hope is God's promise: "Greater is he that is in you, than he that is in the world" (1 John 4:4 KJV).

I don't see a demon hiding behind every tree. I know some people who, when someone sneezes, rebuke the demon of sneezing (or the demon of hiccups)! But I am convinced that an invisible world of spiritual conflict *does* rage around us. Angels and demons battle, and our prayers are an important part of the battle plan.

In our scientific, postmodern culture, "enlightened" people laugh at the idea of demons. In his book *The Screwtape Letters,* C. S. Lewis proposes the idea that every person has a "demon" assigned to them. The book contains letters from a senior devil, Screwtape, to a young novice demon, Wormwood, who has been assigned to tempt and torment his assignment. In one section Screwtape writes, "The fact that 'devils' are predominately comic figures in the modern imagination will help you. If any faint suggestion of your existence begins to arise in his mind, suggest to him a picture of something in red tights, and persuade him that since he cannot believe in that, he therefore cannot believe in you."[3]

Satan and his demons don't demand that you recognize their existence or worship them. In fact, Satan prefers to work incognito, disguised as an angel of light to lead you astray so that you aren't a fully devoted follower of Christ. Satan doesn't mind if you claim to be a Christian and go to church. In fact, he wants you to be proud of that fact. He just doesn't want you to become a sold-out, radical believer—a prayer warrior. Although Satan does not know everything, he's highly organized. He has an intricate network of demon helpers. Demons are not like dogs let loose in a park, chasing butterflies and sniffing the grass. They have a detailed plan. The Devil has a delegation of sinister soldiers who try to influence people in every nation. He stirs up prejudice against the church of Christ, always seeking to resist the spread of the gospel and the building of God's kingdom. That's why prayer is spiritual warfare.

Prayer Is Our Strategic Weapon Against Satan's Strongholds (10:20)

If you desire to have victory in the Christian life, you must learn this dynamic truth about prayer. The spiritual struggle we glimpse in Daniel 10 is real, and it continues today. As we study current world events, Satan and his legions of fallen angels clearly are at work to obstruct the plan of God. Because our greatest weapon is prayer, we can logically expect our greatest opposition when we are on our knees. As Daniel teaches us, the fallen angels do not quit the battle until they must. The price we must pay for victory is persistence—praying until we receive the answer.

An important key in warfare praying is found in 2 Corinthians 10:4–5: "The weapons we fight with are not the weapons of the world [guns, knives, or bombs]. On the contrary, they have divine power to demolish strongholds. We demolish arguments and every pretension that sets itself up against the knowledge of God, and we take captive every thought to make it obedient to Christ."

The biblical word for "stronghold" indicates a "fortress." It is a military word that refers to an area where the enemy is entrenched. In spiritual terms, it means an area of your life where your adversary, the Devil, has discovered a weakness in your spiritual defenses. At your point of weakness he has erected an outpost, a fortress from which he aims his fiery darts at you. A stronghold might be an obsession or some attitude or thought pattern that keeps you from experiencing spiritual victory. Strongholds may be found on the subconscious level. Like an iceberg, perhaps only a small portion of a stronghold may appear above the surface of your consciousness. Strongholds may include worry, anger, hatred, lust, aggression, unreasonable fear, or unrestrained urges and appetites. Many addictions may be the result of a stronghold that the Devil has erected in the mind of a person. The nature of a stronghold isn't nearly as important as *how* you can demolish it. Second Corinthians 10 tells us that we possess spiritual weapons to pull down strongholds, and the most powerful weapon is prayer. The primary place where you will engage in spiritual warfare is in your private prayer time.

According to the Bible, prayer has "divine power to demolish strongholds." Are you using this weapon? Most of our battles are fought in prayer. When we get up off our knees, then we go out to enjoy the spoils of battle!

REVIVAL IN AMERICA

America needs a spiritual awakening—a revival—in the deepest way. What's the answer to the teenage drinking-and-driving problem? Revival. What's the answer to violence and crime? Revival. What's the answer to fractured families where husbands aren't being the spiritual leaders? Revival.

As Christians, we point our fingers of blame at the wicked people in America. However, the problem is not with the pornographer, the bootlegger, the casino operator, or the drug pusher. God said, "*If my people, which are called by my name, shall humble themselves, and pray, and seek my face, . . . then will I hear from heaven, and will forgive their sin, and will heal their land*" (2 Chron. 7:14 KJV, emphasis added). God is waiting for His people, the church, to repent.

In times of prosperity and plenty, it's hard to imagine that God's judgment might fall upon us. We must learn from our history. The early part of the nineteenth century was a time of unprecedented growth and prosperity in America, and then our nation was thrown suddenly into the bloody Civil War. Abraham Lincoln was a student of both Scripture and his culture. In the middle of a bitter war, he issued a "Proclamation of a Day of National Humiliation, Fasting, and Prayer." Lincoln wrote,

> We have been the recipients of the choicest bounties of Heaven; we have been preserved these many years in peace and prosperity; we have grown in numbers, wealth, and power as no nation has ever grown. But we have forgotten the gracious hand, which preserved us in peace; and we have vainly imagined, in the deceitfulness of our hearts, that all these blessings were produced by some superior wisdom and virtue of our own. Intoxicated with unbroken success, we have become too self-sufficient to feel the necessity of God's redeeming and preserving grace—too proud to pray to the God that made us. . . . It behooves us, then, to humble ourselves before the offended Power to confess our national sins and pray clemency and forgiveness upon us.
>
> —President Abraham Lincoln, March 30, 1863

Would you like to change your world? Change your personal chaos into character? Change your nation? The very best way to do it is to pray. Daniel prayed persistently, and God answered him. Are you willing to become a Daniel and pray and confess the national sins of our society? That's the only hope for real revival in our land.

Chapter Nine

Daring to Be a Daniel

In 168 B.C., the Syrian king unleashed a terrible persecution. He killed thousands of Jews and polluted the temple with a pig. During that crisis, the Jews circulated the book of Daniel. As they read it, they found the courage to stay faithful to God. In December 164 B.C., the Jews reclaimed and rededicated the temple (that's what Hanukkah celebrates). In the same way, faithful followers of God in the future will once again read the book of Daniel during a time of terrible persecution at the end of time called the Great Tribulation. As they read it at that time, it will make more sense to them and encourage them more than it does us today! Just as the book of Revelation concludes with a wonderfully encouraging doxology, so does the book of Daniel.

In our fast-paced society, people want to get to "the bottom line." We have coined a lot of phrases to describe this desire. We say, "Cut to the chase," "Don't beat around the bush," and "Just give it to me straight!" Or, as Joe Friday used to say on the TV show *Dragnet,* "Just the facts, ma'am." Daniel 12 contains four bottom-line truths from the Word of God. There's a difference between facts and truth. For instance, 2 + 2 = 4 is a fact, but it doesn't change your life. Jesus said, "I am the way, the truth, and the life . . ." (John 14:6 KJV). That's truth, and it can transform your life. As we examine these four bottom-line truths, I challenge you to ask yourself a personal question in response to each truth.

1. God's Truth: There Is a Book of Life (12:1)

My response: *Is my name written in the Book of Life?*

> At that time Michael, the great prince who protects your people, will arise. There will be a time of distress such as has not happened from the beginning of nations until then [the seven-year Tribulation that will take place after the rapture of the church]. But at that time your people [Israel]—everyone whose name is found written in the book—will be delivered. (Dan. 12:1)

Several times in the Bible we are told that a book in heaven contains the names of selected people. God relates to us as individuals. Your name, which represents your life, is important to God. Perhaps you've had your name written on certain lists here on earth. You might be on the list of "who's who" (or "who's not"). Your name might be listed on the membership rolls of clubs or organizations. You might even have your name on the membership list of a church or Christian fellowship. But the only list of names that matters for eternity is in the Book of Life.

Your pressing concern should be, "Is my name written in the Book of Life?" This list in heaven doesn't necessarily coincide with any church membership list. Churches might offer a false sense of security if they communicate that church membership is synonymous with salvation. I recall visiting a neighboring pastor years ago when I was a young pastor. I saw a membership list for his church lying on his desk. Beside several of the names on each page he had written the letters FBPO. I asked him, "What does FBPO stand for?" He said, "Oh, that means 'For Burial Purposes Only.'

Those are people whose names are on our church roll, but they seldom attend or serve the Lord. The only reason they're a member is so that when they die, their obituary can read that they were a member of a church."

That's an interesting observation. But, it's not our job to decide who is truly saved or not—that's God's job. However, based upon what Jesus said in Matthew 7:21, multitudes of religious people might have their names on a church roll, but they aren't written in God's book. You might ask, "How, then, can I be *sure* my name is written in the Book of Life?" Simple. Do you know Jesus? In Matthew 7:23, Jesus rejects those religious-talking people because He says, "I never *knew* you" (emphasis added). A personal relationship with Jesus ensures that your name is in the Book of Life.

Knowing about Jesus is not the same as knowing Jesus. We all know about George Washington, but none of us knows him. If you've read this book, you probably know about Jesus, but do you know Him? I met Him years ago, and my life has never been the same. I talk to Him several times every day. He speaks to me through His Word. We have a personal, intimate relationship. That's how you can be certain that your name is in God's book.

> As I looked, the thrones were set in place, and the Ancient of Days took his seat. His clothing was as white as snow; the hair of his head was white like wool. His throne was flaming with fire, and its wheels were all ablaze. A river of fire was flowing, coming out from before him. Thousands upon thousands attended him; ten thousand times ten thousand stood before him. The court was seated, and the books were opened. (Dan. 7:9–10)

Who is this "Ancient of Days"? *Ancient* doesn't mean "old" here; it means eternal, ageless, and everlasting. Perhaps this phrase is where some people get the idea that God is an old man with a long, white beard and long, white hair. God isn't old; He's ageless! The Bible says, "From everlasting to everlasting you are God" (Ps. 90:2). Jesus claimed, "I am the Alpha and the Omega. . . . I am the First and the Last" (Rev. 1:8, 17).

The Ancient of Days is a reference to the Eternal God. The description symbolizes His character. White clothing speaks of His purity. White hair has nothing to do with age; it indicates His Holy, sinless nature. Compare this description of God with the one the apostle John saw in Revelation 1:14: "His head and hair were white like wool, as white as snow, and his eyes were like blazing fire."

In Daniel 7:10, we see what's happening in this vision: "A river of fire was flowing, coming out from before him. Thousands upon thousands attended him [probably angels]; ten thousand times ten thousand stood before him. The court [or literally "judgment"] was seated, and the books were opened."

This description of the Final Judgment coincides with the one found in Revelation 20:11–12, 15: "Then I saw a great white throne and him who was seated on it. Earth and sky fled from his presence, and there was no place for them. And I saw the dead, great and small, standing before the throne, and books were opened. Another book was opened, which is the book of life. The dead were judged according to what they had done as recorded in the books. . . . If anyone's name was not found written in the book of life, he was thrown into the lake of fire."

Obviously, Daniel and John are describing the same event—the Final Judgment, which is for those who reject God's offer of eternal life. Children of God won't be there. *Dead* refers to those who are spiritually dead without Christ. The evidence brought against those who refuse God's love will be contained in the "books." The Bible speaks of at least the following three different books.

1. *Book of Works.* Every evil thought, wicked deed, and cor-

rupt word ever spoken will be recorded in this book and then revealed at the judgment. Jesus said in Matthew 12:36, "But I tell you that men will have to give account on the day of judgment for every careless word they have spoken." Not only evil works will be recorded but also everyone's "good works." Many people think that if they perform *more* "good deeds" than "bad deeds," God will let them into heaven. But salvation is "by *grace* . . . through *faith*— . . . not by works, so that no one can boast" (Eph. 2:8–9, emphasis added). These "good works" will simply bear witness to the fact that there are not enough good works in the history of the world to allow someone to earn his or her way into heaven.

2. *The Bible.* In John 12:48 Jesus said, "There is a judge for the one who rejects me and does not accept my words; that very word which I spoke will condemn him at the last day." The Bible will be exhibit A at the last judgment. People will be reminded of every time they heard a Bible verse or read the Bible. That memory will be there to testify that they did not heed the Scripture. The Bible is God's love letter to mankind. Enough truth is available in a single verse (e.g., John 3:16) to take anyone to heaven. The Bible is either the "word of life" that leads one to God or it will one day stand in judgment against them.

3. *The Book of Life.* Jesus told His disciples, "Rejoice that your names are written in heaven" (Luke 10:20). The most important book at the Judgment Day is the Book of Life (Rev. 20:12, 15). When you repent of your sins and trust Jesus alone for salvation, your name is written in the Lamb's Book of Life. The Book of Life will be at the Final Judgment. None of the names of the lost are written in it, so it will be this "absence of evidence" that condemns them.

How horrible it will be for those who stand before God at this Final Judgment! Imagine that standing there is a religious person whom we'll call Bill, who never came to know Jesus. When the recording angel opens the Book of Life, he reports to the Judge that Bill's name is not recorded. Bill says, "Well, check again because I was a member of my church for more than forty years!" The angel confirms that Bill's name is absent. Bill says, "Lord, Lord, I sang in the choir. I took up the offering!" But it's too late then, for Christ Himself said, "Many will say to me on that day, 'Lord, Lord, did we not prophesy in your name, and in your name drive out demons and perform many miracles?' Then I will tell them plainly, 'I never knew you. Away from me, you evildoers!'" (Matt. 7:22–23).

2. God's Truth: There Are Two Future Resurrections (12:2)

My response: *Which resurrection will be mine?*

> Multitudes who sleep in the dust of the earth will awake: some to everlasting life, others to shame and everlasting contempt. (Dan. 12:2)

> A time is coming when all who are in their graves will hear his voice and come out—those who have done good will rise to live, and those who have done evil will rise to be condemned. (John 5:28–29)

> Blessed and holy are those who have part in the first resurrection. The second death has no power over them. (Rev. 20:6)

During Easter, we celebrate the resurrection of Jesus. Although it is a historical fact, the personal meaning of Jesus' resurrection also must be appreciated. None of us is going to live in his or her physical body forever. Our bodies are only temporary. They grow old, get sick, and finally stop. We die. You can exercise, eat properly, tuck it, lift it, move it, or groove it, but the most you can hope for is to add a few more years. But don't worry; death is not the end. Our souls live on. In addition, one day our bodies will be resurrected. The Bible teaches that there will be two resurrections. (Read Revelation 20 to learn more.)

Those whose names are written in the Book of Life will be resurrected to eternal life. We will live with Jesus forever. The Bible never teaches universalism, which is the belief that one day everyone will be saved. Universalism wagers that in the future God will change His mind and say, "I know what I said, but I'm a God of mercy. So why don't all of you come on into heaven?"

Many Scriptures verify that there are two eternal destinies: heaven and hell. Daniel confirmed that some people will be resurrected to eternal life but others to eternal shame and contempt.

The Bible calls hell the "second death" (Rev. 20:14). Physical death is just the "first death." So, there are two births and two deaths in the Bible. We've all had a physical birth, but Jesus said in John 3:7, "You must be born again." This second birth is a spiritual birth that occurs when we trust Jesus.

Because there are two "births" and two "deaths," consider this fact: "If you are born *once,* you'll die *twice.* But if you are born *twice,* you'll only die *once.*" Understand? If you are born once (physically) and then you are never born again (spiritually), you'll die twice. Your first death will be physical, and then in the future your body will be resurrected to go through a second death (the lake of fire). But God loves you and has taken extraordinary measures to show you that He doesn't want that to happen to you. That might be why He brought you to this place to read this paragraph! If you are born twice (both physically and spiritually), you'll die only once (physically), and the "second death" will never touch you.

3. God's Truth: An Explosion of Information Will Characterize the Last Days (12:4)

My response: *Am I recognizing the current signs of the Last Days?*

God delivers a mysterious command to Daniel in 12:4: "But you, Daniel, close up and seal the words of the scroll until the time of the end. Many will go here and there [that speaks of transportation] to increase knowledge [that speaks of information]." These two characteristics describe the "time of the end." Daniel was told that the last days will see an improvement in transportation and an explosion of information.

Isaac Newton has been called the father of modern physics. He was a committed Christian and one of the first scientists to see God's hand in the orderly design of the universe. Harold Wilmington wrote that in 1680 Sir Isaac Newton read these same words in Daniel and commented, "Personally, I cannot help but believe that these words refer to the end of the times. Men will travel from country to country in an unprecedented manner. There may be some inventions which will enable people to travel much more quickly than they do now."[1] Isaac Newton went on to suggest that this speed might exceed fifty miles per hour! When the French atheist Voltaire read that Newton had suggested that people would travel so quickly, he scoffed, "See what a fool Christianity makes of an otherwise brilliant man! Here a scientist like Newton actually writes that men may travel at the rate of forty to fifty miles per hour. Has he forgotten that if a man would travel at this rate he would be suffocated? His heart would stand still!"[2]

The space shuttle astronauts currently travel at speeds in excess of eighteen thousand miles per hour. Daniel was right, and Isaac Newton was on the right track in understanding what Daniel was saying. From Daniel's time (530 B.C.) until a little more than one hundred years ago, the fastest a man could travel was on horseback at a top speed of thirty miles per hour, for short bursts only. During the past one hundred fifty years, we've witnessed the advent of the train, the automobile, the jet, and spacecraft. Until it was recently retired, one could fly from New York City to Paris in three hours on the Concorde.

We are also witnessing a mind-boggling information explosion. Just as the Industrial Age revolutionized the world, the current Information Age is creating changes faster than we can adapt. Never before has so much information been made available to so many people. At this writing, people don't even need a desktop or a laptop to access cyberinformation. I can connect to the Internet on my handheld PDA and cell phone. Computers are smaller and faster and they run everything today. The four most dreaded words in business are *our computers are down*. When that happens, most offices have to close. We have become ever computer dependant.

The amount of information and knowledge is increasing exponentially. That means that it is like a number squared rather than a number multiplied. Someone has observed that from the time Jesus died until 1700, knowledge doubled. It took seventeen hundred years! But then by 1900, after only two hundred years, knowledge doubled again. By 1950, technological information had doubled again, in only fifty years. Then by 1970, there was another doubling—twenty years. Now it is doubling every two years, and if some of the predictions of quantum physics come true, it could double in one day sometime in the near future.

Don't let this technological explosion scare you. To me, it simply proves that the Bible is true and that we are approaching the last days. Although we have advanced far into the Information Age, our culture is still morally bankrupt. In 1948, after America had dropped the atom bombs to end World War II, General Omar Bradley spoke to an audience of scientists in Boston. "We have grasped the mystery of the atom and rejected the Sermon on the Mount," he said. "With the monstrous weapons man already has, humanity is in danger of being trapped in this world by moral adolescents. Our knowledge of science has already outstripped our capacity to control it. We have too many men of science, too few men of God."[3] Although he spoke those words more than fifty years ago, I think they are still true.

What should we do? Jesus said, "Even so, when you see all these things, you know that it is near, right at the door. . . . So you also must be ready, because the Son of Man will come at an hour when you do not expect him" (Matt. 24:33, 44). When we consider Christ's return, we shouldn't set dates or try to calculate the timetable of His coming. Our job is to be faithful to Him and to serve Him by sharing His message with others. We must be even *more* faithful to do this "as [we] see the Day approaching" (Heb. 10:25).

In 12:8, Daniel asked, "What will the outcome of all this be?" God tells him, "Go your way" (v. 9). That meant to keep doing what he'd always done: to pray, to serve, to worship. The angel revealed that the true application of this final portion of the prophecy would be sealed until the end of time. Then the angel predicted in verse 10, "Many will be purified, made spotless and refined, but the wicked will continue to be wicked. None of the wicked will understand, but those who are wise will understand."

We can expect that toward the end of time, chaos will increase, the wicked will get even more wicked (we are certainly seeing that in America), but at the same time, God's people are going to be increasingly more committed to Jesus. I believe we are going to see a dual revival in the last days. I expect to see a remarkable spiritual awakening in the church! But at the same time, there will be a parallel increase in wickedness and sin. As we approach the return of Christ, the spiritual "middle ground" is going to shrink to nothing. People will have to choose to follow Christ faithfully or to reject Him; however, they will not be able to ignore Him.

Some people try to live with one foot in the world and one foot in the kingdom of Jesus. They live two different lifestyles, one for church and another for the rest of the time. As we get closer to the end, this option will disappear. It will be like a boat that is drifting away from the dock. You have one foot on the dock and one foot in the boat, and you have to decide! The boat is moving away, and if you don't decide—splash—you end up all wet! What about Jesus? What will it be for you?

4. God's Truth: There Is Rest and Reward for God's Children (12:13)

My response: *Do I have a personal relationship with God?*

Finally, God offers a personal word to Daniel. Try to picture the faithful saint of God, still on fire for God. He is praying and serving His Lord. God says to Daniel in verse 13, "As for you, go your way till the end [that means just keep doing what you've been doing until you die]. You will rest, and then at the end of the days you will rise to receive your allotted inheritance."

We have no record of when Daniel died, but most likely it was soon after he received this final prophecy. He lived his final days with the assurance that God had promised him rest and an inheritance. This is a good place to ask yourself a couple of questions. "How much longer will I live?" You don't know the answer to *that* question, but you should know the answer to the next one. "Will I live the rest of my life with the assurance that when I die I will spend eternity in heaven with Jesus?" Daniel enjoyed a personal relationship with God. He wasn't just a participant in some religion. He knew the God of the universe. He spoke to Him every day, and God spoke to him.

If you dare to be a Daniel, you'll walk with God and talk with Him daily. If you know Him, here's the promise you can claim:

> *"Blessed are the dead who die in the Lord from now on." "Yes," says the Spirit, "they will rest from their labor, for their deeds will follow them"* (Rev. 14:13).

Endnotes

CHAPTER 3: KEEPING YOUR COOL WHEN THE HEAT IS ON

1. From "Humanist Manifesto II," *The Humanist,* September/October 1973.
2. Stephen Miller, *Daniel,* The New American Commentary, Vol. 18 (Nashville: Broadman and Holman, 1994), 123.

CHAPTER 4: SURRENDERING YOUR LIFESTYLE

1. Francis Thompson (1859–1907), "The Hound of Heaven" (Boston: Branden Publishing Co., June 1978).
2. See Bob Buford, *Halftime: Changing Your Game Plan from Success to Significance* (Grand Rapids: Zondervan, 1994).

CHAPTER 6: FACING THE FUTURE WITHOUT FEAR

1. Ray Stedman, *Discovery Papers,* Vol. 16 (Palo Alto, Calif.: Discovery Publishing), 4.

CHAPTER 7: CONFESSION *Is* GOOD FOR THE SOUL

1. S. D. Gordon, *Quiet Talks on Prayer* (New York: Grosset and Dunlap, 1941), 12.
2. Andrew Murray, *With Christ in the School of Prayer* (Grand Rapids: Zondervan, 1983), 161.
3. Charles Spurgeon, *Sermon Archive,* Metropolitan Tabernacle Pulpit Sermons, London.
4. Chuck Colson with Ellen Santilli Vaughn, *Against the Night: Living in the New Dark Ages* (Ann Arbor, Mich.: Servant, 1989), 11.

CHAPTER 8: SPIRITUAL BATTLE STATIONS

1. David O. Dykes, *Do Angels Really Exist?* (Lafayette, La.: Huntington House, 1996).
2. John Piper, from a message delivered at Bethlehem Baptist Church, Bethlehem, Pennsylvania, 15 August 1996.
3. C. S. Lewis, *The Screwtape Letters* (New York: Macmillan Publishing Co., 1977), letter 7, 33.

CHAPTER 9: DARING TO BE A DANIEL

1. Harold Willmington, *Basic Stages in the Book of Ages* (n.p., 1977), 375.
2. Ibid.
3. Stephen Donadio, ed., *New York Public Library of Twentieth-Century American Quotations* (Lebanon, Ind.: Warner Books, 1992), 367.